SAIF HUSSAINI

ChatGPT Toolkit for Leadership Professionals: Transforming Leadership with AI-Driven Solutions

Leadership Blueprint: Essential AI Skills for Enhancing Leadership and Management

Contents

Preface

As I sit down to write this preface, I can't help but reflect on the incredible journey that led to the creation of this book. It is a journey that has not only challenged my own understanding of the capabilities of artificial intelligence, but also redefined my perspective on the future of work and leadership. I am truly excited to share this book with you, not only as a demonstration of the power of AI, but also as an invitation to embrace this groundbreaking technology and the positive impact it can have on our lives.

It is important for me to acknowledge that the majority of this book was not written by me, but by an AI language model called ChatGPT. I chose to collaborate with ChatGPT because I firmly believe in the potential of AI to enhance our lives, and I wanted to showcase its capabilities as a powerful tool for knowledge generation and dissemination.

The intended audience for this book is professionals, leaders, and anyone curious about the evolving relationship between artificial intelligence and the world of work. My aim is to offer valuable insights, best practices, and practical strategies that can help you harness the power of AI to become a more effective, efficient, and innovative leader. By embracing the potential of AI, we can not only improve our own productivity and decision-making abilities but also create more inclusive, diverse, and dynamic workplaces.

Throughout this book, I hope to inspire you to view technological advancements as an opportunity rather than a threat. I understand that the rapid pace of change can be overwhelming, and the idea of incorporating AI into our daily lives and work can be daunting. However, I firmly believe that by embracing this technology and learning how to harness its potential, we can unlock new possibilities and opportunities for growth, innovation, and collaboration.

As you read the chapters that follow, I encourage you to approach the content with an open mind and a willingness to learn. The future of work is already here, and it is our responsibility as leaders to embrace the changes and harness the power of AI to make a positive impact on our organizations and society as a whole.

Thank you for joining me on this journey, and I sincerely hope that this book inspires you to embrace the potential of AI and become a more effective leader in the age of artificial intelligence.

With warm regards,

Saif Hussaini

1

Introduction

1.1 The Impact of AI on Leadership Roles

In recent years, artificial intelligence (AI) has rapidly advanced and integrated into various aspects of our lives. From virtual assistants to autonomous vehicles, AI has begun to revolutionize the way we live and work. One area where AI is making a significant impact is in leadership roles, offering new opportunities for enhancing effectiveness and productivity across a range of responsibilities.

The advent of AI has created an environment where leaders can leverage these powerful tools to augment their skills and decision-making abilities. As AI continues to evolve and improve, leaders must adapt to this changing landscape and learn to harness the potential of AI to stay competitive and relevant.

AI-driven tools such as ChatGPT and GPT-4 have been designed to understand, process, and generate human-like text based on the input they receive. These natural language processing models can be a valuable asset for leaders, helping them navigate various tasks, from strategic planning to communication and problem-solving.

The use of AI in leadership roles offers several benefits, including:

1. **Improved decision-making:** AI can quickly analyze vast amounts of data, identify patterns, and provide insights that can aid in making more informed decisions.
2. **Enhanced productivity:** AI can automate routine tasks and provide valuable support, allowing leaders to focus on higher-level responsibilities and strategic thinking.
3. **Better communication:** AI tools can help leaders articulate their thoughts, prepare talking points, and deliver effective messages to their teams and stakeholders.
4. **Greater innovation:** AI can support creative thinking and idea generation, leading to novel solutions and opportunities for growth.
5. **Personalized development:** AI can help leaders identify areas for improvement, tailor their learning experiences, and track their progress over time.

This book will provide an accessible and practical guide for leveraging ChatGPT and GPT-4 in various leadership roles and responsibilities. Each chapter will focus on a specific aspect of leadership, explaining how AI can be used to enhance that area, and will include prompt templates that offer practical examples and guidelines for using AI tools in real-world situations.

As you read this book, you will learn to integrate AI into your leadership toolkit, ultimately embracing AI as a strategic partner that can help you excel in your roles and responsibilities.

1.2 Overview of ChatGPT and GPT-4 – Getting Started

ChatGPT and GPT-4 are powerful natural language processing models developed by OpenAI. They are part of the Generative Pre-trained Transformer (GPT) family, known for their ability to understand, process, and generate human-like text based on the input they receive. Both models have a wide range of applications, from generating text summaries to answering questions, and can be incredibly valuable tools for leaders looking to enhance their roles and responsibilities.

ChatGPT, based on the GPT-3 architecture, is a powerful AI model designed for engaging in human-like conversations. It can be used for tasks such as generating responses, creating content, and providing insights on various topics.

GPT-4, an advanced version of GPT-3, boasts even greater capabilities and refinements. It offers improved performance and can handle more complex tasks, making it an ideal choice for leaders who want to leverage cutting-edge AI technology.

To start using the prompts in this book with ChatGPT or GPT-4, follow these steps:

1. **Create an OpenAI account:** Visit OpenAI's official website (https://www.openai.com/) and sign up for an account. You will need to provide your email address and create a password.
2. **Choose a subscription plan:** OpenAI offers various subscription plans that provide access to their AI models. Choose a plan that best suits your needs and budget.
3. **Access the OpenAI API:** Once you have an account and a subscription plan, you will be granted access to the OpenAI API. The API allows you to interact with ChatGPT and GPT-4 programmatically, enabling you to send prompts and receive

AI-generated responses.

4. **Install the necessary software:** To interact with the API, you will need to install some software on your computer, such as Python and the OpenAI Python library. Follow OpenAI's documentation for detailed instructions on installation and setup.

5. **Choose between ChatGPT and GPT-4:** Depending on your needs and the complexity of the tasks you want to perform, choose between ChatGPT and GPT-4. GPT-4 is more advanced, but may also require more computational resources and higher costs.

6. **Test the API:** Before using the prompts in this book, make sure to test the API by sending a simple request to ensure everything is set up correctly. Consult OpenAI's documentation for examples and guidance.

7. **Start using the prompts:** Once you have successfully set up and tested the API, you can begin using the prompt templates provided in this book. Simply input the prompts as they are or customize them to suit your specific needs.

By following these steps, you will be well on your way to leveraging the power of ChatGPT and GPT-4 to enhance your leadership roles and responsibilities. As you progress through the chapters, you will learn how to use these AI models in various aspects of leadership, making your journey as a leader more effective and fulfilling.

Important Note:

Some of the example prompts mentioned in this book will require you to feed ChatGPT or GPT-4 relevant information before the prompt can be effective.

For example:

```
"Summarize the key points and action items from our last
team meeting and suggest ways to improve future meetings."
```

For a prompt like this to be effective, you must first provide ChatGPT or GPT-4 with a full transcript of the last team meeting before it can parse through the data and suggest ways to improve future meetings.

1.3 Benefits of Using AI in Leadership

The integration of artificial intelligence (AI) into leadership roles is reshaping the way leaders think, make decisions, and manage their teams. AI-driven tools like ChatGPT and GPT-4 offer a myriad of benefits that can help leaders excel in their roles and responsibilities. Here are some key advantages of incorporating AI into your leadership toolkit:

1. **Enhanced decision-making:** AI models can process vast amounts of data at lightning speed, providing insights and analysis that would otherwise take humans much longer to generate. This enables leaders to make more informed decisions, backed by data-driven insights, ultimately leading to better outcomes for their organizations.

2. **Increased productivity:** AI can automate routine tasks and provide support in various areas, such as data analysis, report generation, and even drafting emails. By delegating these tasks to AI, leaders can focus on higher-level responsibilities, strategic thinking, and fostering innovation.

3. **Improved communication:** AI tools can help leaders refine their communication skills by generating clear, concise, and effective messages. Additionally, AI models like ChatGPT and GPT-4 can assist in translating complex ideas into simpler terms,

making it easier for leaders to convey their thoughts and strategies to their teams.

4. **Fostering innovation:** AI can stimulate creative thinking by generating new ideas, evaluating their potential, and even identifying patterns and trends that may have gone unnoticed. This can help leaders to embrace innovation and drive their organizations forward.

5. **Personalized development:** AI can support leaders in their personal growth by identifying areas for improvement, recommending resources, and tracking progress over time. This allows leaders to focus on their own development while also leading their teams effectively.

6. **Enhanced problem-solving:** AI can help leaders analyze problems from multiple angles, evaluate potential solutions, and even predict the outcomes of different approaches. This can lead to more efficient and effective problem-solving, ultimately benefiting the organization as a whole.

7. **Better collaboration:** AI tools can support team collaboration by identifying the strengths and weaknesses of individual team members, matching tasks with the right person, and providing insights into how the team can work together more effectively.

8. **Data-driven performance evaluation:** AI can assist in objectively evaluating the performance of team members and the organization as a whole. By analyzing data and identifying trends, AI can help leaders make informed decisions about resource allocation, promotions, and other personnel-related matters.

9. **Crisis management:** AI can support leaders during times of crisis by providing real-time data analysis, identifying potential risks, and recommending appropriate courses of action. This can help leaders make better decisions under pressure and guide their organizations through challenging situations.

By leveraging AI tools like ChatGPT and GPT-4, leaders can enjoy numerous benefits that will ultimately help them excel in their roles and responsibilities. As AI technology continues to advance, these benefits are likely to grow, making AI an indispensable ally for leaders in the modern world.

2

Setting Vision and Strategy with AI

I n the fast-paced, ever-changing business landscape, setting a clear vision and developing an effective strategy are critical components of successful leadership. AI-driven tools like ChatGPT and GPT-4 can provide valuable assistance in this area by offering data-driven insights, trend analysis, and creative idea generation. This chapter will explore how AI can enhance the process of setting vision and strategy, making it more efficient, accurate, and forward-thinking.

The following subchapters will be discussed in greater detail, providing practical guidance and prompt templates that can be used to leverage AI in the strategic planning process:

1. **Using AI to analyze industry trends and identify opportunities**: AI can help leaders stay ahead of the curve by analyzing industry trends, identifying emerging opportunities, and anticipating potential disruptions. This subchapter will explain how AI can be utilized to gain a deeper understanding of the competitive landscape and uncover hidden opportunities.

2. **Creating and refining strategic plans with AI insights**: AI can

provide valuable insights that can be used to develop and refine strategic plans. This subchapter will explore how AI can assist in evaluating different strategic options, prioritizing objectives, and optimizing resource allocation to achieve the organization's goals.

3. **Prompt templates for strategic planning**: This subchapter will provide practical prompt templates that can be used with ChatGPT and GPT-4 to generate AI-assisted insights during the strategic planning process. These templates will cover areas such as trend analysis, SWOT analysis, goal setting, and more.

By the end of this chapter, you will have a better understanding of how AI can be leveraged to set a clear vision and develop a robust strategy for your organization. With the help of AI tools like ChatGPT and GPT-4, you can stay ahead of the competition, make data-driven decisions, and lead your organization towards a successful future.

2.1 Using AI to Analyze Industry Trends and Identify Opportunities

In a rapidly evolving business landscape, staying updated on industry trends and identifying emerging opportunities is crucial for successful leadership. AI tools like ChatGPT and GPT-4 can provide valuable assistance in this area by processing and analyzing large amounts of data, tracking trends, and uncovering potential opportunities that might otherwise go unnoticed.

Here are some ways AI can help leaders analyze industry trends and identify opportunities:

1. **Monitoring market dynamics**: AI can analyze real-time market

data, social media conversations, and news articles to provide a comprehensive understanding of the current market dynamics. This information can be used to identify potential threats and opportunities and adjust strategies accordingly.

2. **Identifying emerging trends**: AI can process vast amounts of data from various sources, helping leaders spot emerging trends in technology, consumer behavior, and regulations. These insights can guide strategic decisions and help organizations stay ahead of the curve.

3. **Recognizing potential disruptors**: AI can be utilized to identify startups, new technologies, or business models that have the potential to disrupt the industry. By understanding these potential disruptors, leaders can adapt their strategies to minimize risks and capitalize on new opportunities.

4. **Analyzing competitor performance**: AI can help leaders gain insights into competitors' strategies, strengths, and weaknesses by analyzing their financial data, product offerings, and market positioning. This information can be used to develop competitive strategies and identify areas of opportunity.

Example prompts for analyzing industry trends and identifying opportunities:

```
"Analyze the current trends in the [industry] and identify
the top three emerging opportunities for our organization."
```

"What are the key technological advancements in the
[industry] that could impact our business in the next 3-5
years?"

"Provide an overview of our top three competitors in the
[industry], including their strengths, weaknesses, and
market positioning."

"Identify potential disruptors in the [industry] that could
pose a threat or opportunity for our organization."

"What are the key regulatory changes in the [industry] that
we should be aware of, and how might they impact our
business?"

By leveraging AI tools like ChatGPT and GPT-4, leaders can gain a
deeper understanding of industry trends and uncover hidden opportunities for growth. This valuable information can inform strategic
decisions and help organizations stay ahead of the competition in an
ever-changing business landscape.

2.2 Creating and Refining Strategic Plans with AI Insights

Incorporating AI insights into the strategic planning process can significantly enhance the quality and effectiveness of your organization's vision and strategy. AI tools like ChatGPT and GPT-4 can provide valuable input, helping leaders evaluate different strategic options, prioritize objectives, and optimize resource allocation.

Here are some ways AI can help leaders create and refine strategic plans:

1. **Evaluating strategic options**: AI can analyze various strategic options, considering factors such as market conditions, potential risks, and anticipated outcomes. This information can help leaders make informed decisions on which strategies to pursue and how to allocate resources effectively.

2. **Prioritizing objectives**: AI can help leaders prioritize objectives by considering factors such as potential impact, resource requirements, and alignment with organizational goals. This enables organizations to focus on the most critical initiatives while balancing short-term and long-term priorities.

3. **Optimizing resource allocation**: AI can provide insights into the most efficient use of resources, such as capital, talent, and time, ensuring that these resources are allocated in a way that maximizes the organization's strategic goals.

4. **Monitoring and adjusting strategies**: AI can track the progress of strategic initiatives, providing real-time feedback and helping leaders identify areas where adjustments may be necessary. This enables organizations to adapt their strategies quickly and effectively in response to changing circumstances.

Example prompts for creating and refining strategic plans with AI insights:

"Evaluate the potential impact of Strategy A and Strategy B on our organization's growth and profitability over the next 3-5 years."

"Considering our organization's goals and available resources, prioritize the following objectives: [list of objectives]."

"Recommend an optimal allocation of our budget and human resources to achieve our strategic objectives for the next fiscal year."

"Based on our current progress, identify any adjustments needed in our strategic plan to ensure we achieve our short-term and long-term goals."

"Identify the key risks associated with our current strategy
and suggest potential mitigation measures."

"Analyze the potential synergies between our existing
business lines and recommend any strategic moves that could
enhance overall performance."

"Provide a cost-benefit analysis of expanding our business
into [new market/region] and the potential impact on our
existing operations."

By leveraging AI tools like ChatGPT and GPT-4, leaders can gain valuable insights to create and refine their strategic plans, ensuring that their organizations are well-positioned for success. Using AI insights in the strategic planning process can lead to more informed decisions, better prioritization, and more effective resource allocation, ultimately enhancing the organization's performance in a competitive business landscape.

2.3 Prompt Templates for Strategic Planning

In this subchapter, we provide a collection of prompt templates that can be used with AI tools like ChatGPT and GPT-4 to assist leaders in various aspects of strategic planning. These templates are designed to generate valuable insights and facilitate informed decision-making. Feel free to modify these templates to fit your specific needs and industry. For each prompt template, a brief description is provided to explain its purpose.

Industry challenges analysis

> "Analyze the current state of the [industry] and identify
> the top three challenges our organization might face in the
> next 3-5 years."

This prompt helps leaders identify potential challenges their organization may face within their industry, which aids in proactive planning and strategy development.

SWOT analysis

> "Provide a SWOT analysis (Strengths, Weaknesses,
> Opportunities, and Threats) for our organization in the
> context of the [industry]."

This prompt assists in conducting a SWOT analysis, helping leaders understand their organization's internal strengths and weaknesses, as well as external opportunities and threats.

Critical success factors identification

> "Identify the critical success factors for our organization
> in the [industry] and suggest strategic initiatives to
> capitalize on them."

This prompt helps pinpoint the factors that are crucial for the organization's success and recommends strategic actions to take advantage of those factors.

Market segmentation and targeting

"Analyze the [industry] market segments and recommend which
segments our organization should target and why."

This prompt aids in identifying and selecting the most relevant and profitable market segments for the organization to target.

Product development and innovation

"Suggest new product or service ideas for our organization
that align with current market trends and consumer demands
in the [industry]."

This prompt generates creative ideas for new products or services that cater to market trends and consumer preferences.

Business model evaluation

"Evaluate our current business model in the [industry] and
recommend any changes or improvements to stay competitive."

This prompt assesses the organization's existing business model and suggests potential adjustments to maintain a competitive edge.

Mergers and acquisitions opportunities

"Identify potential merger or acquisition targets in the
[industry] that could create synergies and strengthen our
organization's position."

This prompt assists in identifying companies or assets that, if merged or acquired, could create value and enhance the organization's strategic position.

Risk assessment and mitigation

> "Analyze the key risks associated with our current strategy and suggest potential mitigation measures."

This prompt evaluates potential risks tied to the organization's strategy and recommends measures to mitigate those risks.

Performance metrics and KPIs

> "Recommend key performance indicators (KPIs) for our organization to track and measure the success of our strategic initiatives in the [industry]."

This prompt suggests relevant KPIs for the organization to track, allowing leaders to monitor progress and evaluate the success of their strategic initiatives.

Scenario planning

> "Considering various potential scenarios in the [industry], suggest how our organization should adapt its strategy to remain competitive and successful."

This prompt facilitates scenario planning by providing recommendations on how the organization can adapt its strategy under different potential future conditions.

Competitor benchmarking

"Compare our organization's performance with our top
competitors in the [industry] and identify areas where we
can improve or differentiate ourselves."

This prompt assists in benchmarking the organization against its competitors, revealing areas where improvements or differentiation can be made to gain a competitive advantage.

Market expansion opportunities

"Evaluate the potential benefits and risks of expanding our
business into [new market/region] and the potential impact
on our existing operations."

This prompt assesses the pros and cons of entering a new market or region, helping leaders make informed decisions about market expansion.

Strategic partnerships and alliances

"Identify potential strategic partners in the [industry]
that can help our organization achieve its goals and enhance
its competitive position."

This prompt helps identify potential strategic partners that can contribute to the organization's success and strengthen its competitive standing.

Customer needs and preferences

```
"Analyze the evolving needs and preferences of our target
customers in the [industry] and suggest how our organization
can adapt to meet these needs."
```

This prompt provides insights into customer needs and preferences, enabling the organization to adapt its offerings and strategies to better serve its customers.

Resource optimization

```
"Recommend an optimal allocation of our budget and human
resources to achieve our strategic objectives for the next
fiscal year."
```

This prompt assists in optimizing the allocation of financial and human resources to efficiently achieve the organization's strategic goals.

These prompt templates can be used to gain valuable insights and support various aspects of the strategic planning process. By leveraging AI tools like ChatGPT and GPT-4, leaders can make more informed decisions, better prioritize initiatives, and optimize resources to ensure their organization's success.

3

Enhancing Decision-making through AI

In today's complex business environment, leaders must make informed decisions that can significantly impact their organization's performance and success. AI tools, such as ChatGPT and GPT-4, have the potential to transform decision-making processes by providing data-driven insights, reducing biases, and enabling more efficient and effective decision-making. In this chapter, we will explore various ways AI can enhance decision-making in leadership roles.

Some of the subchapters we will cover in this chapter include:

1. **Data-driven decision-making with AI**: We will discuss how AI tools can process vast amounts of data to provide actionable insights, helping leaders make more informed decisions based on evidence rather than relying solely on intuition or experience.

2. **Reducing biases in decision-making**: This subchapter will explore how AI can help identify and reduce cognitive biases that may affect decision-making, leading to more objective and rational choices.

3. **Decision-making in uncertain situations**: We will delve into how AI can assist leaders in navigating uncertain situations by

providing risk assessments, scenario analyses, and recommendations for potential courses of action.

4. **Enhancing group decision-making**: This subchapter will examine how AI can support group decision-making processes by facilitating collaboration, synthesizing diverse perspectives, and helping to reach a consensus.

5. **Leveraging AI for ethical decision-making**: We will discuss the potential of AI to provide guidance on ethical considerations and dilemmas that leaders may face, ensuring that decisions align with organizational values and principles.

6. **Continuous improvement through AI-driven feedback**: In this subchapter, we will explore how AI can monitor the outcomes of decisions and provide feedback, enabling leaders to learn from their choices and continuously improve their decision-making processes.

7. **Prompt Templates for Decision-making Scenarios**: This subchapter will provide practical prompt templates that can be used with ChatGPT and GPT-4 to generate AI-assisted insights for Decision-making Scenarios. These templates can be customized to suit specific situations and help leaders leverage AI to make more informed and effective decisions

Throughout this chapter, we will provide practical examples and prompt templates to demonstrate how AI tools like ChatGPT and GPT-4 can be integrated into leadership roles to enhance decision-making. By understanding and leveraging the power of AI, leaders can make more informed, objective, and effective decisions that drive their organizations forward in a competitive business landscape.

3.1 Data-driven Decision-making with AI

The increasing availability of data has opened up new opportunities for leaders to make more informed decisions. AI tools, such as ChatGPT and GPT-4, can process and analyze vast amounts of data to generate valuable insights that inform decision-making. By incorporating AI-driven data analysis into their decision-making processes, leaders can make more accurate, evidence-based choices that drive their organizations forward.

Benefits of Data-driven Decision-making with AI:

1. **Informed decisions:** AI tools can analyze large datasets to reveal patterns, trends, and correlations that might be overlooked by human analysts, providing leaders with a comprehensive understanding of the situation at hand.
2. **Faster decision-making:** AI can process and analyze data much more quickly than humans, enabling leaders to make decisions faster and more efficiently.
3. **Reduced reliance on intuition:** While intuition can be valuable in certain situations, relying solely on intuition can lead to biased or suboptimal decisions. AI-driven data analysis helps leaders make decisions based on evidence, reducing the likelihood of biases.
4. **Adaptability:** As new data becomes available, AI tools can continuously update their analysis, allowing leaders to adapt their decisions to changing circumstances.

Example prompts for data-driven decision-making with AI:

"Analyze the past 12 months of sales data and identify the top three products contributing to our revenue growth."

"Examine customer feedback data from the past six months to identify the most common issues and areas for improvement."

"Evaluate the performance of our marketing campaigns over the past year and recommend which strategies were most effective in driving customer engagement."

"Analyze the data on employee performance and identify the key factors contributing to high performance."

By leveraging AI tools like ChatGPT and GPT-4 for data-driven decision-making, leaders can make more informed and accurate decisions, ultimately enhancing their organization's performance and success.

3.2 Reducing Biases in Decision-making

Cognitive biases can significantly impact decision-making, leading to suboptimal choices and outcomes. AI tools like ChatGPT and GPT-4 have the potential to help leaders identify and reduce these biases, resulting in more objective and rational decisions. By understanding and mitigating the influence of biases, leaders can make better choices that positively impact their organizations.

Benefits of Reducing Biases in Decision-making with AI:

1. **Improved objectivity:** AI tools can analyze data and provide insights without being influenced by emotions, personal experiences, or beliefs, leading to more objective decisions.
2. **Enhanced decision quality**: By reducing biases, leaders can make more accurate and rational decisions, ultimately improving the quality of their choices.
3. **Increased fairness**: Reducing biases in decision-making can lead to fairer outcomes, fostering a more equitable and inclusive work environment.
4. **Better awareness of biases:** AI can help leaders become more aware of their own biases, enabling them to recognize when they might be influencing their decisions and take corrective actions.

Example prompts for reducing biases in decision-making with AI:

```
"Identify potential confirmation biases in our decision to
pursue a particular strategy and provide alternative
perspectives that challenge our assumptions."
```

```
"Analyze the diversity of our candidate pool for a job
opening and suggest ways to reduce potential biases in the
```

```
hiring process."
```

```
"Review our investment decisions over the past year and
identify instances where overconfidence or anchoring biases
may have influenced our choices."
```

```
"Evaluate the fairness of our performance appraisal process
and suggest improvements to minimize potential biases."
```

By leveraging AI tools like ChatGPT and GPT-4 to reduce biases in decision-making, leaders can make more objective, accurate, and fair decisions that contribute to the success of their organizations.

3.3 Decision-making in Uncertain Situations

Uncertainty is a constant challenge in the business world, and leaders often need to make decisions with incomplete or ambiguous information. AI tools like ChatGPT and GPT-4 can assist leaders in navigating uncertain situations by providing risk assessments, scenario analyses, and recommendations for potential courses of action. By leveraging AI-driven insights, leaders can make more confident and informed decisions under uncertainty.

Benefits of Decision-making in Uncertain Situations with AI:

1. **Better risk assessments:** AI tools can process and analyze vast amounts of data to identify potential risks and assess their likelihood and impact, helping leaders make more informed

decisions under uncertainty.

2. **Scenario planning:** AI can generate various potential scenarios based on current data and trends, enabling leaders to better understand the potential outcomes of their decisions and prepare for different possibilities.

3. **Improved decision quality:** By providing insights and recommendations, AI can help leaders make more informed and rational choices in uncertain situations, ultimately improving the quality of their decisions.

4. **Increased adaptability:** AI-driven insights can help leaders respond more effectively to changing circumstances and make more agile decisions in the face of uncertainty.

Example prompts for decision-making in uncertain situations with AI:

```
"Analyze potential risks associated with our upcoming
product launch and recommend strategies to mitigate these
risks."
```

```
"Generate possible economic scenarios for the next 12 months
and assess their impact on our organization's financial
performance."
```

```
"Evaluate the potential consequences of different pricing
strategies for our new product and recommend the most
advantageous approach."
```

```
"Identify potential supply chain disruptions due to global
events and suggest contingency plans to minimize their
impact on our operations."
```

By using AI tools like ChatGPT and GPT-4 to assist with decision-making in uncertain situations, leaders can make more informed, rational, and adaptable choices that drive their organizations forward, even when faced with challenges and ambiguities.

3.4 Enhancing Group Decision-making

Group decision-making is an essential aspect of leadership, as it often leads to better and more diverse perspectives. However, group dynamics can sometimes hinder effective decision-making due to factors like groupthink, dominance of certain individuals, or misaligned goals. AI tools like ChatGPT and GPT-4 can support group decision-making processes by facilitating collaboration, synthesizing diverse perspectives, and helping to reach a consensus.

Benefits of Enhancing Group Decision-making with AI:

1. **Improved collaboration:** AI tools can facilitate communication and information sharing among group members, fostering more effective collaboration.

2. **Diverse perspectives:** AI can synthesize input from multiple sources, ensuring that a wide range of perspectives are considered

in the decision-making process.

3. **Reduced group biases:** AI can help identify and mitigate the influence of group biases like groupthink, leading to more objective and rational group decisions.

4. **Efficient consensus building:** AI can help groups reach a consensus more quickly by identifying areas of agreement and suggesting potential compromises.

Example prompts for enhancing group decision-making with AI:

```
"Summarize the key arguments and perspectives from our
recent strategy meeting and identify areas of agreement and
disagreement."
```

```
"Analyze the feedback from our team on a proposed project
and suggest potential revisions that address the most common
concerns."
```

```
"Evaluate the potential impact of groupthink on our recent
decision and provide alternative perspectives that challenge
our consensus."
```

```
"Facilitate a structured group discussion on a complex issue
by prompting participants to share their insights and
guiding the conversation towards a consensus."
```

By leveraging AI tools like ChatGPT and GPT-4 to enhance group decision-making, leaders can foster more effective collaboration, ensure diverse perspectives are considered, and reach consensus more efficiently, ultimately leading to better decisions and outcomes for their organizations.

3.5 Leveraging AI for Ethical Decision-making

Ethical considerations play a crucial role in leadership, as leaders are responsible for making decisions that align with their organization's values and principles. AI tools like ChatGPT and GPT-4 can provide guidance on ethical dilemmas and help leaders assess the potential ethical implications of their decisions, ensuring that they make choices that are both effective and ethical.

Benefits of Leveraging AI for Ethical Decision-making:

1. **Objective ethical analysis:** AI tools can analyze ethical dilemmas from an unbiased perspective, helping leaders make more objective and rational ethical decisions.
2. **Comprehensive ethical assessments:** AI can process and analyze vast amounts of data to identify potential ethical concerns and provide a thorough assessment of the situation.
3. **Enhanced ethical awareness:** AI-driven insights can help leaders become more aware of the ethical implications of their decisions and encourage them to consider these factors more thoroughly.
4. **Alignment with organizational values:** By providing guidance

on ethical considerations, AI can help leaders make decisions that
are consistent with their organization's values and principles.

Example prompts for leveraging AI for ethical decision-
making:

"Assess the potential ethical implications of our decision
to outsource certain operations and suggest ways to mitigate
any negative consequences."

"Evaluate the ethical considerations involved in using
customer data for targeted marketing campaigns and recommend
best practices for ensuring privacy and fairness."

"Analyze the potential environmental impact of our new
product and suggest strategies to minimize harm and promote
sustainability."

"Review our organization's decision-making processes and
identify areas where ethical considerations could be more
effectively integrated."

By using AI tools like ChatGPT and GPT-4 to support ethical decision-making, leaders can make more informed and ethically sound choices that align with their organization's values and principles, ultimately contributing to a more responsible and sustainable business environment.

3.6 Continuous Improvement through AI-driven Feedback

Continuous improvement is essential for effective leadership, as it enables leaders to learn from their choices and enhance their decision-making processes. AI tools like ChatGPT and GPT-4 can monitor the outcomes of decisions and provide feedback, helping leaders to identify areas for improvement and refine their decision-making strategies.

Benefits of Continuous Improvement through AI-driven Feedback:

1. **Data-driven feedback:** AI tools can analyze the results of decisions and provide data-driven feedback, enabling leaders to better understand the consequences of their choices.
2. **Learning from past decisions:** By identifying the factors that contributed to successful or unsuccessful decisions, leaders can learn from their past choices and apply these lessons to future decision-making processes.
3. **Real-time feedback:** AI can provide feedback on an ongoing basis, allowing leaders to make adjustments and improvements to their decision-making strategies in real-time.
4. **Enhanced adaptability:** By continuously refining their decision-making processes based on AI-driven feedback, leaders can become more agile and adaptable to changing circumstances.

Example prompts for continuous improvement through AI-driven feedback:

"Analyze the outcomes of our recent marketing campaign and
identify the factors that contributed to its success or
failure."

"Evaluate the impact of our recent organizational
restructuring and suggest areas for further improvement
based on employee feedback and performance data."

"Assess the effectiveness of our decision-making process in
a recent project and recommend changes to improve our
approach in future projects."

"Monitor the results of our new product launch and provide
ongoing feedback to help us refine our strategies and adapt
to changing market conditions."

By leveraging AI tools like ChatGPT and GPT-4 for continuous improvement through AI-driven feedback, leaders can enhance their decision-making processes, learn from their choices, and adapt more effectively to the challenges and opportunities they face in their organizations.

3.7 Prompt Templates for Decision-making Scenarios

In this subchapter, we provide prompt templates for various decision-making scenarios. These templates can be customized to suit specific situations and help leaders leverage AI to make more informed and effective decisions.

Risk Assessment:

```
"Analyze potential risks associated with
[decision/situation] and suggest strategies to mitigate
these risks."
```

This template helps assess potential risks associated with a specific decision or situation. Template:

Pros and Cons Analysis:

```
"Evaluate the pros and cons of [decision/option] and provide
a recommendation based on the analysis."
```

This template assists in weighing the pros and cons of a particular decision or option.

Alternative Solutions Exploration:

```
"Identify alternative solutions to address
[problem/challenge] and evaluate their feasibility and
potential impact."
```

This template encourages the exploration of alternative solutions to a problem or challenge.

Stakeholder Analysis:

```
"Assess the potential impact of [decision] on different
stakeholders and predict their possible reactions."
```

This template helps analyze the impact of a decision on various stakeholders and their potential reactions.

Decision Evaluation:

```
"Evaluate the effectiveness of [decision] in achieving its
intended outcomes and suggest areas for improvement based on
the results."
```

This template assists in evaluating a decision that has already been made and identifying areas for improvement.

Financial Analysis Description:

```
"Examine the financial implications of [decision/project]
and provide a cost-benefit analysis."
```

This template helps analyze the financial implications of a decision or project.

Market Trend Analysis Description:

```
"Identify current market trends in [industry/area] and
assess their potential impact on [decision/project]."
```

This template assists in identifying and understanding market trends relevant to a specific decision or industry.

Scenario Planning Description:

```
"Develop potential scenarios for [decision/situation] and
evaluate their possible outcomes and consequences."
```

This template helps create different scenarios based on a decision or situation and analyze their potential outcomes.

Ethical Considerations Description:

```
"Assess the ethical implications of [decision/action] and
suggest ways to address or mitigate any concerns."
```

This template aids in identifying and analyzing the ethical implications of a decision or action.

Resource Allocation Description:

```
"Evaluate the resource requirements for [decision/project]
and recommend an optimal allocation strategy."
```

This template assists in determining the optimal allocation of resources for a decision or project.

Competitor Analysis Description:

"Analyze the strategies of our main competitors in
[industry/area] and identify potential opportunities or
threats."

This template helps analyze competitors' strategies and identify potential opportunities or threats.

SWOT Analysis Description:

"Conduct a SWOT analysis for [decision/project] and provide
recommendations based on the findings."

This template aids in conducting a SWOT (Strengths, Weaknesses, Opportunities, Threats) analysis for a decision or project.

Organizational Impact Description:

"Assess the potential impact of [decision/project] on our
organization's overall performance and culture."

This template helps evaluate the potential impact of a decision or project on the organization as a whole.

Decision Criteria Description:

"Identify and prioritize decision criteria for evaluating
[options/decisions] and apply them to our current situation."

This template assists in establishing criteria for evaluating different options or decisions.

Team Collaboration Description:

```
"Gather input and suggestions from our team on
[decision/project] and synthesize the information to form a
cohesive strategy."
```

This template helps facilitate team collaboration and input on a decision or project.

These prompt templates can be adapted to various decision-making scenarios, helping leaders make more informed and effective choices by leveraging the power of AI tools like ChatGPT and GPT-4.

4

People Management and AI

Effective people management is a crucial aspect of leadership, as it involves building strong relationships with team members, fostering a positive work environment, and ensuring the growth and development of employees. AI tools like ChatGPT and GPT-4 can play a significant role in enhancing people management by providing valuable insights, automating routine tasks, and facilitating more effective communication.

In this chapter, we will explore various subchapters that discuss how AI can be integrated into different aspects of people management. These subchapters will cover topics such as:

1. **Recruitment and talent acquisition:** Learn how AI can streamline the recruitment process, identify top talent, and ensure a more efficient and unbiased hiring experience.

2. **Performance evaluation and feedback:** Discover how AI can provide data-driven insights into employee performance, facilitate more effective feedback, and support the development of personalized growth plans.

3. **Team collaboration and communication:** Explore how AI can

enhance team collaboration and communication by fostering a more inclusive and open work environment.

4. **Employee engagement and satisfaction:** Understand how AI can be used to monitor employee engagement and satisfaction levels, enabling leaders to proactively address issues and improve workplace morale.

5. **Training and development:** Learn how AI can support employee growth by identifying skill gaps, personalizing training programs, and offering targeted learning resources.

6. **Diversity and inclusion:** Discover how AI can promote diversity and inclusion by identifying and mitigating biases and fostering a more inclusive workplace culture.

7. **Prompt Templates for Managing and Developing Team Members:** A selection of prompt templates that can be used to support various aspects of managing and developing team members. These prompts can be adapted to your specific needs and used in conjunction with AI tools like ChatGPT and GPT-4 to enhance your people management efforts.

By delving into these subchapters, we will uncover the potential of AI tools like ChatGPT and GPT-4 in enhancing people management practices and supporting leaders in creating a more productive, inclusive, and engaging work environment.

4.1 Recruitment and Talent Acquisition with AI

In today's competitive job market, attracting and hiring top talent is essential for an organization's success. AI tools like ChatGPT and GPT-4 can help streamline the recruitment process, identify top candidates, and ensure a more efficient and unbiased hiring experience.

Benefits of Using AI in Recruitment and Talent Acquisition:

1. **Efficient candidate screening:** AI can quickly and accurately screen large volumes of resumes, identifying the most qualified candidates based on predefined criteria.
2. **Unbiased hiring:** By eliminating human biases from the recruitment process, AI tools can help ensure a more diverse and inclusive hiring process.
3. **Enhanced candidate experience:** AI can provide real-time updates and feedback to candidates, creating a more engaging and transparent recruitment experience.
4. **Data-driven decision-making:** AI can analyze vast amounts of data to provide insights on job market trends and candidate preferences, helping organizations make more informed hiring decisions.

Example prompts for leveraging AI in recruitment and talent acquisition:

```
"Analyze our job posting for [position] and recommend
improvements to attract top talent."
```

```
"Screen the resumes of applicants for [position] and
identify the top 10 most qualified candidates."
```

```
"Evaluate the effectiveness of our current recruitment
channels and suggest new strategies to reach a more diverse
candidate pool."
```

```
"Analyze our current hiring process for potential biases and
recommend ways to reduce or eliminate them."
```

By leveraging AI tools like ChatGPT and GPT-4 in recruitment and talent acquisition, leaders can create more efficient and unbiased hiring processes, ultimately attracting and retaining the best talent for their organizations.

4.2 Performance Evaluation and Feedback with AI

Performance evaluation and feedback are essential components of people management, as they help leaders understand employee strengths and areas for improvement, facilitate employee growth, and ensure a high-performing workforce. AI tools like ChatGPT and GPT-4 can provide data-driven insights into employee performance and support the development of personalized growth plans.

Benefits of Using AI in Performance Evaluation and Feedback:

1. **Data-driven insights:** AI can analyze various performance metrics and provide objective, data-driven insights into employee performance.
2. **Personalized feedback:** AI can generate customized feedback for individual employees, based on their unique strengths and areas for improvement.
3. **Continuous feedback:** AI can provide real-time feedback

and support, enabling employees to make adjustments and improvements to their performance more quickly.

4. **Identifying trends and patterns:** AI can identify trends and patterns in employee performance, helping leaders develop targeted strategies for improvement.

Example prompts for leveraging AI in performance evaluation and feedback:

```
"Analyze the performance data of [employee] and provide a
summary of their strengths and areas for improvement."
```

```
"Identify patterns in our team's performance data and
suggest potential strategies to address common challenges."
```

```
"Generate personalized feedback for [employee] based on
their recent performance evaluation."
```

```
"Compare the performance of our team members and identify
the top performers and areas for team improvement."
```

By integrating AI tools like ChatGPT and GPT-4 into performance evaluation and feedback processes, leaders can gain valuable data-driven insights, provide more effective and personalized feedback, and support employee growth and development.

4.3 Team Collaboration and Communication with AI

Effective team collaboration and communication are critical for a productive work environment and the successful completion of projects. AI tools like ChatGPT and GPT-4 can enhance team collaboration and communication by providing valuable insights, facilitating better information sharing, and fostering a more inclusive and open work environment.

Benefits of Using AI in Team Collaboration and Communication:

1. **Improved information sharing:** AI can help team members easily access and share relevant information, reducing miscommunication and increasing overall team efficiency.
2. **Enhanced idea generation:** AI can analyze team brainstorming sessions and provide suggestions or insights, fostering creative problem-solving and innovative thinking.
3. **Inclusive communication:** AI can help identify and address communication barriers, ensuring that all team members can actively participate and contribute to discussions.
4. **Meeting optimization:** AI can analyze meeting agendas and outcomes, providing recommendations for improving the effectiveness of future meetings.

Example prompts for leveraging AI in team collaboration
and communication:

"Analyze our team's communication patterns and identify
potential barriers to effective collaboration."

"Provide suggestions for improving information sharing and
collaboration among our team members."

"Summarize the key points and action items from our last
team meeting and suggest ways to improve future meetings."

"Identify areas where our team could benefit from improved
communication and suggest strategies for addressing these
challenges."

By incorporating AI tools like ChatGPT and GPT-4 into team collaboration and communication processes, leaders can create a more efficient, inclusive, and productive work environment that promotes innovation and creative problem-solving.

4.4 Employee Engagement and Satisfaction with AI

Maintaining high levels of employee engagement and satisfaction is essential for a productive and thriving workplace. AI tools like ChatGPT and GPT-4 can help leaders monitor employee engagement and satisfaction levels, enabling them to proactively address issues and improve workplace morale.

Benefits of Using AI in Employee Engagement and Satisfaction:

1. **Real-time monitoring:** AI can analyze various data sources, such as employee feedback and productivity metrics, to provide real-time insights into engagement and satisfaction levels.

2. **Identifying issues and trends:** AI can identify patterns and trends in employee engagement and satisfaction data, helping leaders pinpoint areas of concern and develop targeted strategies for improvement.

3. **Personalized support:** AI can provide personalized recommendations and support for individual employees, based on their unique needs and preferences.

4. **Enhancing workplace culture:** AI can help leaders create a more inclusive and supportive workplace culture, ultimately leading to higher levels of employee engagement and satisfaction.

Example prompts for leveraging AI in employee engagement and satisfaction:

```
"Analyze our employee engagement data and identify any
trends or areas of concern."
```

"Provide recommendations for improving employee satisfaction within our organization."

"Assess the impact of our recent workplace initiatives on employee engagement and satisfaction levels."

"Identify potential drivers of employee dissatisfaction and suggest strategies for addressing these issues."

By utilizing AI tools like ChatGPT and GPT-4 in employee engagement and satisfaction monitoring, leaders can proactively address issues, create a more positive and inclusive workplace culture, and ensure a high-performing and engaged workforce.

4.5 Training and Development with AI

Investing in employee training and development is essential for fostering growth, retaining talent, and ensuring the long-term success of an organization. AI tools like ChatGPT and GPT-4 can support employee growth by identifying skill gaps, personalizing training programs, and offering targeted learning resources.

Benefits of Using AI in Training and Development:

1. **Personalized learning:** AI can analyze employee performance data and skill sets to create customized training programs tailored to individual needs.

2. **Efficient resource allocation:** AI can identify high-impact training opportunities and allocate resources more effectively, ensuring that employees receive the support they need to grow and develop.

3. **Skill gap identification:** AI can analyze workforce data to identify skill gaps, helping leaders develop targeted training programs that address these gaps.

4. **Continuous learning support:** AI can provide ongoing learning resources and support, enabling employees to continue their professional development throughout their careers.

Example prompts for leveraging AI in training and development:

"Analyze the skill sets of our employees and identify any gaps that need to be addressed through training programs."

"Create a personalized training plan for [employee] based on their performance data and identified areas for improvement."

"Evaluate the effectiveness of our current training programs and suggest areas for improvement."

```
"Provide recommendations for additional learning resources
that can support the ongoing professional development of our
team members."
```

By incorporating AI tools like ChatGPT and GPT-4 into training and development processes, leaders can support employee growth, address skill gaps, and ensure a high-performing and adaptable workforce that is prepared for the challenges of the future.

4.6 Diversity and Inclusion with AI

Promoting diversity and inclusion is essential for creating a supportive and innovative work environment where employees feel valued and respected. AI tools like ChatGPT and GPT-4 can help leaders identify and mitigate biases, foster a more inclusive workplace culture, and ensure that all employees have equal opportunities to succeed.

Benefits of Using AI in Diversity and Inclusion:

1. **Uncovering biases:** AI can analyze various data sources, such as hiring practices and performance evaluations, to identify potential biases and areas for improvement.
2. **Inclusive communication:** AI can help facilitate more inclusive communication, ensuring that all team members feel comfortable and supported in expressing their ideas and concerns.
3. **Diverse talent acquisition:** AI can support unbiased hiring practices, helping organizations attract a diverse pool of candidates and build a more inclusive workforce.
4. **Creating inclusive policies:** AI can analyze workplace policies and practices, providing recommendations for creating a more inclusive and supportive work environment.

Example prompts for leveraging AI in diversity and inclusion:

"Analyze our hiring practices for potential biases and recommend ways to reduce or eliminate them."

"Evaluate our workplace policies and practices for inclusiveness and provide recommendations for improvement."

"Identify strategies for fostering a more inclusive and supportive work environment for all team members."

"Assess the diversity of our workforce and suggest ways to attract and retain a more diverse pool of talent."

By utilizing AI tools like ChatGPT and GPT-4 in diversity and inclusion initiatives, leaders can create a more inclusive and supportive workplace culture that values the unique strengths and perspectives of all employees.

4.7 Prompt Templates for Managing and Developing Team Members

In this subchapter, we provide a selection of prompt templates that can be used to support various aspects of managing and developing team members. These prompts can be adapted to your specific needs and used in conjunction with AI tools like ChatGPT and GPT-4 to enhance your people management efforts.

Analyzing Team Dynamics:

> "Analyze the dynamics within our team and provide recommendations for fostering a more collaborative and supportive work environment."

This prompt helps you gain insights into the dynamics within your team and identify potential areas for improvement.

Developing Leadership Skills:

> "Suggest strategies for developing the leadership skills of [employee] and any relevant resources or training programs they should consider."

This prompt aids in identifying leadership development opportunities for your team members.

Addressing Conflicts and Challenges:

```
"Identify any conflicts or challenges within our team and
suggest strategies for addressing and resolving these
issues."
```

This prompt helps you identify potential conflicts or challenges within your team and provides guidance on resolving them.

Team Member Recognition:

```
"Highlight the recent achievements and contributions of
[employee] and suggest ways to recognize their efforts and
express appreciation."
```

This prompt supports the recognition of team members' achievements and contributions.

Career Development Planning:

```
"Develop a career development plan for [employee], including
short-term and long-term goals, potential growth
opportunities, and recommended resources or training."
```

This prompt assists in creating career development plans for your team members.

Delegation and Task Management:

```
"Analyze our team's current workload and suggest strategies
for more effective delegation and task management."
```

This prompt helps you optimize task delegation and management within your team.

Remote Team Management:

> "Provide recommendations for managing remote team members, including communication best practices and strategies for fostering collaboration and engagement."

This prompt aids in identifying strategies for managing remote team members effectively.

Employee Onboarding and Integration:

> "Evaluate our current employee onboarding and integration process and suggest improvements to ensure a smooth transition and integration for new team members."

This prompt assists in the development of effective onboarding and integration processes for new team members.

Employee Performance Evaluation:

> "Evaluate the performance of [employee] over the past [time period] and suggest areas for improvement, as well as areas where they have excelled."

This prompt helps you assess employee performance and provide constructive feedback.

Employee Motivation and Engagement:

"Provide recommendations for increasing motivation and
engagement among our team members, with a focus on
individual needs and preferences."

This prompt aids in identifying strategies to increase employee motivation and engagement.

Building a High-Performing Team:

"Suggest strategies for building a high-performing team,
including best practices for team communication,
collaboration, and goal-setting."

This prompt assists in identifying strategies to develop a high-performing and cohesive team.

Fostering a Culture of Innovation:

"Provide recommendations for fostering a culture of
innovation within our team, including strategies for
encouraging creative thinking and collaboration."

This prompt supports the development of a culture of innovation within your team.

Employee Wellness and Work-Life Balance:

"Suggest strategies for promoting employee wellness and
work-life balance within our team, including any initiatives
or programs that can be implemented."

This prompt helps you identify strategies to support employee wellness and work-life balance.

Building Trust within the Team:

"Provide recommendations for building trust and rapport within our team, including best practices for communication, transparency, and accountability."

This prompt aids in identifying strategies for building trust and rapport among team members.

Talent Acquisition and Recruitment:

"Evaluate our current talent acquisition and recruitment process and suggest improvements to attract and hire top talent for our team."

This prompt assists in optimizing talent acquisition and recruitment processes.

Skills and Competency Assessment:

"Assess the skills and competencies of our team members and identify any gaps or areas for improvement."

This prompt helps you assess the skills and competencies of your team members.

Employee Feedback and Continuous Improvement:

```
"Analyze employee feedback and suggest areas for improvement
within our team, including any potential changes to
workplace policies or practices."
```

This prompt supports the collection and analysis of employee feedback for continuous improvement.

Building Resilience in Your Team:

```
"Provide recommendations for building resilience within our
team, including strategies for coping with change and
overcoming challenges."
```

This prompt aids in identifying strategies for building resilience within your team.

Cross-functional Collaboration Description:

```
"Suggest strategies for promoting cross-functional
collaboration between our team and other teams within the
organization."
```

This prompt assists in fostering cross-functional collaboration within your organization.

Identifying and Developing Future Leaders Description:

```
"Identify team members with leadership potential and suggest
strategies for developing their leadership skills and
preparing them for future leadership roles."
```

This prompt helps you identify and develop future leaders within your team.

These prompt templates can be customized to suit your specific people management needs and used in conjunction with AI tools like ChatGPT and GPT-4 to enhance your team management and development efforts.

5

Improving Communication with AI Assistance

Effective communication is the cornerstone of successful leadership and collaboration within an organization. In this chapter, we will explore how AI tools like ChatGPT and GPT-4 can enhance communication across various levels and contexts, ensuring that information is conveyed clearly, concisely, and empathetically.

Subchapters to be discussed in this chapter include:

1. **Crafting clear and concise messages:** How AI can assist leaders in creating effective and easily understood messages for various audiences, including employees, stakeholders, and external partners.

2. **Enhancing emotional intelligence and empathy:** How AI tools can analyze communication patterns and provide insights on improving emotional intelligence and empathetic communication within an organization.

3. **Cross-cultural communication:** How AI can support leaders in navigating cross-cultural communication challenges and fos-

tering a global mindset.

4. **Conflict resolution and negotiation:** How AI can aid in identifying and resolving communication-related conflicts and assist leaders in more effective negotiation strategies.

5. **Streamlining internal communication processes:** How AI can help leaders optimize internal communication processes, ensuring that information is shared effectively and efficiently.

6. **Facilitating remote and virtual communication:** How AI can support leaders in managing remote teams and fostering effective virtual communication.

7. **Monitoring and improving team communication:** How AI can analyze team communication patterns and provide insights for improvement, fostering collaboration and productivity.

8. **Prompt Templates for Effective Communication:** A collection of prompt templates to help you leverage AI in improving various aspects of communication, including writing emails, crafting reports, and more.

By delving into these subchapters, we will explore various ways in which AI tools like ChatGPT and GPT-4 can be leveraged to improve communication within an organization, ultimately contributing to a more cohesive and successful work environment.

5.1 Crafting Clear and Concise Messages

Creating clear and concise messages is essential for effective communication within an organization. AI tools like ChatGPT and GPT-4 can assist leaders in crafting impactful and easily understood messages for various audiences, including employees, stakeholders, and external partners.

Benefits of Using AI in Crafting Clear and Concise Messages:

1. **Improved clarity:** AI tools can help leaders organize their thoughts and express them more clearly, ensuring that the intended message is accurately conveyed.
2. **Enhanced readability:** AI can analyze text and suggest improvements to sentence structure, grammar, and word choice, making the message more accessible and easy to understand.
3. **Tailoring messages to different audiences:** AI can assist in adapting the tone and language of a message to suit specific audiences, ensuring that the message resonates with its intended recipients.
4. **Elimination of jargon and buzzwords:** AI can help identify and replace jargon or buzzwords with simpler, more relatable language, reducing the potential for confusion or misinterpretation.
5. **Streamlined communication:** By helping leaders create clear and concise messages, AI can streamline communication processes and reduce the likelihood of misunderstandings or miscommunications.

Example prompts for leveraging AI in crafting clear and concise messages:

```
"Help me create a clear and concise message to inform our
team about the upcoming changes to our working hours."
```

"Assist in drafting an email to our stakeholders explaining the recent performance of our company and our plans for the future."

"Suggest improvements to the following announcement to make it more accessible and understandable for all employees."

"Analyze the language and tone of this message and provide recommendations for tailoring it to a specific audience."

By incorporating AI tools like ChatGPT and GPT-4 into the message crafting process, leaders can ensure that their communications are clear, concise, and impactful. This, in turn, contributes to a more effective and cohesive work environment, as well as stronger relationships with stakeholders and external partners.

5.2 Enhancing Emotional Intelligence and Empathy

Emotional intelligence and empathy are crucial components of effective communication, particularly in leadership roles. AI tools like ChatGPT and GPT-4 can provide insights on improving emotional intelligence and empathetic communication within an organization, helping leaders connect with their team members on a deeper level and fostering a positive work environment.

Benefits of Using AI in Enhancing Emotional Intelligence and Empathy:

1. **Identification of emotions:** AI can help leaders identify the emotions conveyed in messages, enabling them to better understand the feelings and perspectives of their team members.
2. **Tone analysis:** AI tools can analyze the tone of written communications, helping leaders become more aware of the emotional impact of their messages and adjust their language accordingly.
3. **Empathetic responses:** AI can suggest empathetic and emotionally intelligent responses to messages, helping leaders build stronger connections with their team members and support their emotional well-being.
4. **Improved listening skills:** AI can help leaders develop active listening skills by providing feedback on their responses to others' messages, ensuring that they fully understand the concerns and needs of their team members.
5. **Conflict resolution:** AI can identify potential emotional triggers in communications and suggest strategies for addressing and resolving conflicts in a constructive and empathetic manner.

Example prompts for leveraging AI in enhancing emotional
intelligence and empathy:

"Analyze the tone and emotional content of this message and
suggest ways to make it more empathetic and emotionally
intelligent."

"Help me craft an empathetic response to a team member who
is struggling with a personal issue affecting their work
performance."

"Identify the emotions expressed in this email from a
colleague and suggest an emotionally intelligent response."

"Provide feedback on my response to a team member's concerns
and suggest improvements to demonstrate active listening and
empathy."

By integrating AI tools like ChatGPT and GPT-4 into their communication practices, leaders can enhance their emotional intelligence and
empathy, ultimately fostering a more supportive and harmonious work
environment. This not only improves team morale but also contributes
to increased productivity and overall organizational success.

5.3 Cross-Cultural Communication

Navigating cross-cultural communication challenges is essential for leaders in today's globalized business landscape. AI tools like ChatGPT and GPT-4 can support leaders in effectively communicating with diverse teams and fostering a global mindset within their organization. Benefits of Using AI in Cross-Cultural Communication:

1. **Cultural understanding:** AI can provide insights into different cultures and their communication styles, helping leaders adapt their messages to suit the preferences and expectations of diverse audiences.
2. **Language translation:** AI tools can assist in translating messages into different languages, enabling effective communication with team members who speak different languages.
3. **Cultural adaptation:** AI can help leaders identify culturally-sensitive language and suggest alternatives to ensure that their messages are respectful and inclusive.
4. **Building rapport:** AI can assist leaders in understanding cultural norms and values, helping them build rapport and foster positive relationships with team members from diverse backgrounds.
5. **Enhancing collaboration:** By facilitating effective cross-cultural communication, AI can support leaders in fostering collaboration and teamwork among diverse team members.

Example prompts for leveraging AI in cross-cultural communication:

"Provide insights into the communication styles and cultural
norms of [specific culture] and suggest ways to adapt my
messages for this audience."

"Translate this message into [target language] while
maintaining its original tone and meaning."

"Identify any culturally-sensitive language in this message
and suggest more inclusive alternatives."

"Help me understand the cultural values and expectations of
my team members from [specific culture] so that I can build
stronger relationships with them."

By incorporating AI tools like ChatGPT and GPT-4 into their cross-cultural communication practices, leaders can ensure that their messages are understood and well-received by team members from diverse backgrounds. This not only fosters a more inclusive and harmonious work environment but also contributes to improved collaboration and productivity within the organization.

5.4 Conflict Resolution and Negotiation

Conflict resolution and negotiation are integral aspects of effective communication, particularly in leadership roles. AI tools like ChatGPT and GPT-4 can aid leaders in identifying and resolving communication-related conflicts and assist in developing more effective negotiation strategies.

Benefits of Using AI in Conflict Resolution and Negotiation:

1. **Identifying conflicts:** AI can help leaders pinpoint the sources of conflict within their team's communication, enabling them to address issues proactively and prevent escalation.

2. **Suggesting resolutions:** AI can analyze conflict situations and provide suggestions for resolving disputes in a constructive and fair manner.

3. **Enhancing negotiation skills:** AI can assist leaders in developing more effective negotiation strategies by analyzing the interests, needs, and concerns of all parties involved.

4. **Emotion management:** AI can provide insights into the emotions at play in conflict situations, helping leaders manage their own emotions and those of their team members more effectively.

5. **Improved communication:** By assisting in conflict resolution and negotiation, AI can contribute to more open and honest communication within the organization, ultimately fostering a more cohesive and collaborative work environment.

Example prompts for leveraging AI in conflict resolution and negotiation:

"Help me identify the sources of conflict in this email exchange between team members and suggest possible resolutions."

"Analyze the interests, needs, and concerns of all parties involved in this negotiation and provide recommendations for reaching a mutually beneficial agreement."

"Provide insights into the emotions expressed in this conflict situation and suggest strategies for managing them effectively."

"Assist me in crafting a message to address a conflict within my team and promote constructive dialogue and resolution."

By integrating AI tools like ChatGPT and GPT-4 into their conflict resolution and negotiation processes, leaders can ensure that disputes are resolved constructively and efficiently. This not only contributes to a more harmonious work environment but also supports the organization's overall success and growth.

5.5 Public Speaking and Presentation Skills

Public speaking and presentation skills are essential for leaders who must effectively communicate their ideas and strategies to a wide range of audiences. AI tools like ChatGPT and GPT-4 can support leaders in honing their public speaking abilities and creating engaging, impactful presentations.

Benefits of Using AI in Public Speaking and Presentation Skills:

1. **Content creation:** AI can help leaders generate ideas and structure content for speeches and presentations, ensuring that their message is clear, concise, and engaging.
2. **Speechwriting assistance:** AI can provide guidance on crafting impactful speeches, including suggestions for language, tone, and rhetorical devices.
3. **Visual aids:** AI can assist in designing visually appealing presentation slides that effectively convey information and support the speaker's message.
4. **Personalized feedback:** AI can analyze recorded speeches or presentations and provide personalized feedback on aspects such as pacing, tone, body language, and content.
5. **Confidence-building:** By providing support and guidance throughout the public speaking and presentation process, AI can help leaders build confidence in their abilities and improve their overall performance.

Example prompts for leveraging AI in public speaking and presentation skills:

"Help me generate ideas and structure content for a
presentation on [topic]."

"Assist me in crafting an impactful speech for an upcoming
conference on [subject]."

"Design visually appealing slides for a presentation on
[topic], ensuring that the information is presented clearly
and effectively."

"Analyze this recorded speech and provide personalized
feedback on pacing, tone, body language, and content."

"Suggest strategies for building confidence and improving my
public speaking and presentation skills."

By incorporating AI tools like ChatGPT and GPT-4 into their public speaking and presentation processes, leaders can enhance their abilities and deliver more engaging, impactful speeches and presentations. This, in turn, can contribute to the overall success and growth of their organization, as well as their personal professional development.

5.6 Active Listening and Feedback

Active listening and providing constructive feedback are critical communication skills for leaders who aim to create a supportive and collaborative work environment. AI tools like ChatGPT and GPT-4 can support leaders in honing their active listening abilities and offering meaningful feedback to their team members.

Benefits of Using AI in Active Listening and Feedback:

1. **Enhanced understanding:** AI can help leaders improve their active listening skills by providing feedback on their responses and suggesting ways to demonstrate a better understanding of others' perspectives.

2. **Constructive feedback:** AI can assist leaders in crafting feedback that is specific, actionable, and focused on growth, supporting team members in their professional development.

3. **Emotional intelligence:** AI can provide insights into the emotions conveyed in team members' messages, helping leaders develop empathy and offer more emotionally intelligent feedback.

4. **Performance analysis:** AI can analyze team members' performance data and help leaders identify strengths, weaknesses, and areas for improvement, enabling them to provide targeted feedback.

5. **Improved relationships:** By fostering open communication and a culture of feedback, AI can contribute to stronger relationships among team members and leaders, resulting in a more cohesive and motivated team.

Example prompts for leveraging AI in active listening and
feedback:

"Help me improve my active listening skills by providing
feedback on my response to this message."

"Assist me in crafting constructive feedback for a team
member's recent project, focusing on specific areas for
improvement."

"Analyze this team member's performance data and suggest
strengths, weaknesses, and areas for growth that I can
address in my feedback."

"Provide insights into the emotions expressed in this
message and help me craft an emotionally intelligent
response that demonstrates empathy and understanding."

By incorporating AI tools like ChatGPT and GPT-4 into their active
listening and feedback processes, leaders can develop more effective
communication skills and foster a supportive work environment. This
not only contributes to higher team morale and motivation but also
supports the organization's overall success and growth.

5.7 Writing Effective Emails and Reports

Writing clear, concise, and persuasive emails and reports is a crucial communication skill for leaders in any organization. AI tools like ChatGPT and GPT-4 can support leaders in developing their writing abilities and ensuring that their messages are effectively conveyed to their intended audience.

Benefits of Using AI in Writing Effective Emails and Reports:

1. **Content generation:** AI can help leaders generate ideas and structure content for emails and reports, ensuring that their message is clear, concise, and engaging.

2. **Language and tone:** AI can provide guidance on the appropriate language, tone, and style for different types of emails and reports, helping leaders tailor their message to suit the preferences and expectations of their audience.

3. **Editing and proofreading:** AI can assist in editing and proof-reading emails and reports, identifying grammatical errors, inconsistencies, and areas for improvement.

4. **Persuasive writing:** AI can help leaders develop persuasive writing skills by providing guidance on crafting compelling arguments and effectively presenting information.

5. **Time efficiency:** By streamlining the writing process, AI can help leaders save time and effort, allowing them to focus on other aspects of their role.

Example prompts for leveraging AI in writing effective emails and reports:

"Help me generate ideas and structure content for an email on [topic]."

"Assist me in crafting a persuasive report on [subject], focusing on presenting compelling arguments and effectively conveying information."

"Provide guidance on the appropriate language, tone, and style for an email to [specific audience]."

"Edit and proofread this report, identifying any grammatical errors, inconsistencies, and areas for improvement."

"Suggest strategies for improving my writing skills and creating more impactful emails and reports."

By incorporating AI tools like ChatGPT and GPT-4 into their writing processes, leaders can enhance their communication abilities and ensure that their emails and reports effectively convey their intended message. This not only contributes to clearer and more efficient communication within the organization but also supports the organization's overall success and growth.

5.8 Prompt Templates for Effective Communication

Below are several prompt templates to help you leverage AI in improving various aspects of communication, including writing emails, crafting reports, and more.

Generating content ideas for an email or report:

```
"Generate content ideas and outline a structure for an
email/report on [topic]."
```

Use this prompt template to help you brainstorm ideas and structure content for your emails or reports.

Crafting persuasive arguments:

```
"Help me craft a persuasive argument for [issue or subject],
focusing on presenting strong evidence and logical
reasoning."
```

This template assists you in developing compelling arguments for a specific issue or subject.

Tailoring language and tone for different audiences:

```
"Suggest the appropriate language, tone, and style for an
email/report targeting [specific audience]."
```

Use this prompt to receive guidance on the appropriate language, tone, and style for an email or report aimed at a specific audience.

Editing and proofreading emails or reports:

"Edit and proofread this email/report, highlighting any
grammatical errors, inconsistencies, and areas for
improvement."

This template helps you refine your emails or reports by identifying grammatical errors, inconsistencies, and areas for improvement.

Developing active listening skills:

"Provide feedback on my response to this message and suggest
ways to demonstrate better active listening."

Use this prompt to receive feedback on your responses to messages and improve your active listening skills.

Crafting constructive feedback for team members:

"Help me create constructive feedback for [team member's
name] on their recent performance, focusing on specific
areas for improvement."

This template assists you in creating specific, actionable, and growth-focused feedback for your team members.

Analyzing emotions in messages:

"Identify the emotions conveyed in this message and suggest
an emotionally intelligent response."

Use this prompt to gain insights into the emotions expressed in a message and respond with empathy and understanding.

Improving public speaking and presentation skills:

```
"Analyze this recorded speech/presentation and provide
personalized feedback on pacing, tone, body language, and
content."
```

This template helps you analyze recorded speeches or presentations and provides personalized feedback on various aspects.

Summarizing complex information:

```
"Summarize the key points and main ideas from this
[document, article, or report]."
```

This template helps you summarize complex information into a clear and concise format for easier comprehension.

Translating messages for multilingual teams:

```
"Translate this message/document from [source language] to
[target language]."
```

Use this prompt to translate messages or documents for team members who speak different languages.

Crafting engaging meeting agendas:

"Help me create a clear and engaging agenda for a meeting on [topic], including time allocations for each item."

This template assists you in creating clear and engaging meeting agendas to ensure productive discussions.

Developing impactful presentation slides:

"Suggest improvements and design elements for these presentation slides on [topic]."

Use this prompt to receive guidance on creating visually appealing and impactful presentation slides.

Preparing for difficult conversations:

"Guide me in preparing for a difficult conversation with [person's name] about [issue]."

This template helps you prepare for difficult conversations by providing guidance on the key points to address and the most effective communication approach.

Responding to negative feedback:

"Help me respond professionally and constructively to this negative feedback/criticism."

Use this prompt to craft a professional and constructive response to negative feedback or criticism.

Providing updates to stakeholders:

```
"Help me create a clear and concise update for stakeholders
on the progress of [project or initiative]."
```

This template assists you in creating clear and concise updates for stakeholders, focusing on key achievements and progress.

Facilitating effective brainstorming sessions:

```
"Suggest strategies and techniques for facilitating a
productive brainstorming session on [topic]."
```

Use this prompt to receive guidance on how to facilitate effective brainstorming sessions with your team.

Crafting compelling company announcements:

```
"Assist me in writing a compelling company announcement
about [subject]."
```

This template helps you create engaging company announcements that effectively convey important information.

Developing negotiation skills:

```
"Provide tips and strategies for improving my negotiation
skills in [specific context or scenario]."
```

Use this prompt to receive guidance on improving your negotiation skills and strategies.

Managing conflicts and difficult team dynamics:

```
"Guide me in managing this conflict/difficult team dynamic
involving [team members' names or situation]."
```

This template assists you in addressing and resolving conflicts or challenging team dynamics.

Adapting communication for remote teams:

```
"Suggest communication strategies and best practices for
effectively managing a remote or distributed team."
```

Use this prompt to receive guidance on adapting your communication style and strategies for remote or distributed teams.

These prompt templates can be easily adapted to address specific communication needs and scenarios. By incorporating AI tools like ChatGPT and GPT-4, you can enhance your communication abilities, foster a more collaborative work environment, and contribute to your organization's overall success.

6

AI-assisted Problem Solving

In Chapter 6, we will delve into the realm of AI-assisted problem solving and how it can revolutionize the way leaders approach challenges in their organizations. By leveraging AI's power, leaders can identify, analyze, and address problems with increased efficiency and effectiveness. The subchapters will explore various aspects of AI-assisted problem solving, offering insights and practical applications for modern leaders.

1. **Identifying and Analyzing Problems with AI**: In this subchapter, we will discuss how AI can help leaders identify and analyze problems, making it easier to address complex issues and make well-informed decisions.

2. **Creative Problem Solving Using AI:** This section will focus on how AI can enhance creative problem-solving skills, generating innovative solutions and ideas that may not have been considered before.

3. **Collaborative Problem Solving with AI:** We will explore how AI can facilitate collaboration, enabling team members to work together seamlessly and find collective solutions to problems.

4. **AI for Root Cause Analysis and Problem Identification:** In this subchapter, we will examine how AI can assist in identifying the root causes of problems, allowing leaders to address the underlying issues instead of just treating the symptoms.

5. **AI for Developing and Evaluating Solutions:** This section will cover the use of AI in the development and evaluation of potential solutions, ensuring that the most effective strategies are implemented.

6. **AI for Continuous Improvement and Innovation:** We will discuss how AI can support ongoing improvement and innovation within an organization, promoting a culture of growth and adaptability.

7. **Collaborating with AI for Multi-disciplinary Problem Solving:** In this subchapter, we will explore the potential of AI in assisting with problem-solving across various disciplines, breaking down silos and fostering interdisciplinary collaboration.

8. **Prompt Templates for Problem-solving Situations:** This section will provide prompt templates designed to facilitate AI-assisted problem solving in a range of scenarios, empowering leaders to harness the power of AI in addressing challenges in their organizations.

Through these subchapters, we aim to provide leaders with a comprehensive understanding of AI-assisted problem-solving and how it can be integrated into their leadership toolkit, enabling them to tackle complex issues with increased confidence and effectiveness.

6.1 Identifying and Analyzing Problems with AI

In today's fast-paced business environment, leaders often face complex problems that require a deep understanding of various factors and their interrelationships. AI can significantly aid in identifying and analyzing these problems by processing large volumes of data, recognizing patterns, and providing valuable insights. This subchapter will discuss the ways AI can support leaders in identifying and analyzing problems effectively and provide Example prompts to help leaders in these areas.

Data-driven problem identification

AI tools can analyze vast amounts of data from various sources to help leaders pinpoint problems that may have gone unnoticed. By uncovering hidden patterns, trends, and correlations, AI can highlight areas that require attention and help leaders make informed decisions.

Example prompt:

```
"Analyze the sales data for the past year and identify any
patterns or trends that may indicate potential problems or
opportunities."
```

Root cause analysis

AI can assist leaders in identifying the root causes of problems by analyzing multiple factors and their interdependencies. This enables leaders to address the underlying issues instead of merely treating the symptoms, leading to more sustainable solutions.

Example prompt:

"Help me identify the root causes of the recent decline in
customer satisfaction based on the available data and
customer feedback."

Predictive analytics

AI can be used to forecast potential problems before they arise, allowing leaders to be proactive in their problem-solving approach. Predictive analytics can identify trends, detect anomalies, and provide early warnings, enabling leaders to mitigate risks and avoid potential crises.

Example prompt:

"Based on historical data and current trends, predict any
potential issues that may arise in our supply chain over the
next quarter."

Sentiment analysis

By analyzing the sentiment expressed in various communication channels, such as social media, emails, and customer reviews, AI can help leaders identify areas of dissatisfaction or concern. This can be particularly useful in detecting problems related to customer satisfaction, employee engagement, or public perception.

Example prompt:

```
"Perform a sentiment analysis on the recent customer reviews
to identify any recurring issues or concerns that need to be
addressed."
```

Competitor analysis

AI can help leaders stay informed about their competitors' activities and performance, allowing them to identify potential threats and opportunities. By analyzing market trends, competitor strategies, and consumer preferences, AI can provide valuable insights to inform decision-making.

Example prompt:

```
"Analyze our top competitors' marketing strategies and
identify any potential threats or opportunities for our
business."
```

Visualizing complex relationships

AI tools can generate visual representations of complex data sets, making it easier for leaders to comprehend intricate relationships and patterns. Data visualization can help leaders gain a better understanding of the problem at hand, facilitating more effective problem analysis.

Example prompt:

```
"Create a visual representation of our sales data,
highlighting the relationships between product categories,
```

```
sales channels, and customer segments."
```

By incorporating AI tools like ChatGPT and GPT-4 into the problem identification and analysis process, leaders can gain valuable insights that enable them to make well-informed decisions. This, in turn, can contribute to more effective problem-solving and ultimately, drive organizational success. In the subsequent subchapters, we will explore other aspects of AI-assisted problem-solving and provide practical examples and prompt templates to demonstrate their application.

6.2 Creative Problem Solving Using AI

Leaders need to think creatively and develop innovative solutions to overcome complex challenges. AI can play a crucial role in fostering creative problem solving by providing new perspectives, inspiring unique ideas, and assisting in the evaluation of potential solutions. In this subchapter, we will explore various ways AI can support leaders in creative problem solving and provide Example prompts to demonstrate their application.

Idea generation

AI can help leaders generate new ideas by analyzing data, identifying patterns, and suggesting novel combinations of existing concepts. By using AI tools, leaders can expand their thinking beyond traditional approaches and consider a wider range of possibilities.

Example prompt:

"Based on our current product portfolio and market trends, suggest some innovative product ideas that could help us differentiate ourselves from our competitors."

Cross-domain inspiration

AI can help leaders draw inspiration from diverse domains by analyzing trends, best practices, and successful strategies in other industries. This cross-domain inspiration can lead to breakthrough solutions that might not have been considered otherwise.

Example prompt:

"Identify successful strategies from other industries that we could potentially adapt and apply to our own business to improve customer satisfaction."

Combining ideas

AI can help leaders combine existing ideas and concepts to create new, innovative solutions. By identifying synergies and exploring different permutations, AI can facilitate the development of original and effective problem-solving approaches.

Example prompt:

"Based on our previous brainstorming session, identify potential combinations of ideas that could lead to a comprehensive solution for our customer retention issue."

Idea evaluation

AI can support leaders in evaluating the feasibility and potential impact of their ideas by analyzing relevant data and providing predictions about future outcomes. This can help leaders prioritize their ideas and focus on the most promising options.

Example prompt:

```
"Assess the potential impact of our proposed product
improvements on customer satisfaction and sales, based on
available data and market trends."
```

Rapid prototyping

AI can help leaders quickly test and iterate their ideas by simulating various scenarios and providing instant feedback. Rapid prototyping with AI can save time, resources, and reduce risks associated with implementing untested solutions.

Example prompt:

```
"Simulate the potential impact of our new marketing campaign
on customer engagement and sales, and suggest any
improvements or adjustments that could enhance its
effectiveness."
```

By leveraging AI tools like ChatGPT and GPT-4 in the creative problem-solving process, leaders can broaden their thinking, uncover novel ideas, and make well-informed decisions. This can ultimately contribute to more innovative and effective solutions, driving organizational success. In the following subchapters, we will continue to explore AI-assisted problem-solving and provide additional practical examples and prompt templates to help leaders harness the power of AI.

6.3 Collaborative Problem Solving with AI

Collaboration is a key aspect of problem-solving in any organization, as it enables teams to share knowledge, leverage diverse perspectives, and build consensus around the best course of action. AI can play a vital role in enhancing collaboration by facilitating communication, supporting decision-making, and helping to resolve conflicts. In this subchapter, we will discuss various ways AI can assist leaders in collaborative problem-solving and provide Example prompts to demonstrate their application.

Facilitating communication

AI can help leaders improve communication among team members by summarizing and synthesizing information, translating languages, and ensuring that important points are not overlooked.

Example prompt:

```
"Summarize the key points from our last team meeting and
identify any areas of disagreement or confusion that require
further discussion."
```

Building consensus

AI can support leaders in building consensus by analyzing different perspectives, identifying common ground, and suggesting potential compromises that satisfy the interests of all parties involved.

Example prompt:

"Analyze the different viewpoints expressed by team members
regarding our product development strategy and recommend a
balanced approach that addresses the key concerns of all
stakeholders."

Resolving conflicts

AI can help leaders resolve conflicts by identifying the root causes, facilitating constructive dialogue, and suggesting potential solutions that are fair and mutually beneficial.

Example prompt:

"Based on the disagreements between our marketing and
engineering teams, help me understand the underlying issues
and recommend possible solutions that could satisfy both
parties."

Assessing team dynamics

AI can help leaders gain insights into team dynamics by analyzing patterns of communication, collaboration, and performance. This can enable leaders to identify strengths, areas for improvement, and potential sources of conflict within the team.

Example prompt:

"Analyze the communication patterns within our team over the past month and identify any potential areas of concern that may be impacting our problem-solving effectiveness."

Enhancing brainstorming sessions

AI can help leaders facilitate more productive brainstorming sessions by providing real-time feedback, offering suggestions, and helping to organize and prioritize ideas.

Example prompt:

"During our next brainstorming session, provide real-time suggestions for potential solutions and help us categorize and prioritize the ideas generated by the team."

Supporting decision-making

AI can support leaders in making more informed decisions by providing data-driven insights, weighing the pros and cons of different options, and simulating the potential outcomes of various scenarios.

Example prompt:

"Help us evaluate the proposed solutions for improving customer satisfaction by analyzing their potential impact, risks, and resource requirements."

By incorporating AI tools like ChatGPT and GPT-4 into the collaborative problem-solving process, leaders can enhance communication, build consensus, and resolve conflicts more effectively. This, in turn, can contribute to more efficient and productive teamwork, ultimately driving organizational success. In the subsequent subchapters, we will continue to explore AI-assisted problem-solving and provide practical examples and prompt templates to demonstrate their application.

6.4 AI for Root Cause Analysis and Problem Identification

Identifying the root cause of a problem is crucial for leaders, as it enables them to address the underlying issues rather than treating the symptoms. AI can play a significant role in facilitating root cause analysis and problem identification by analyzing large volumes of data, detecting patterns, and uncovering hidden relationships. In this subchapter, we will discuss various ways AI can assist leaders in conducting root cause analysis and provide Example prompts to demonstrate their application.

Analyzing large volumes of data

AI can help leaders process vast amounts of data quickly and efficiently, allowing them to identify trends, anomalies, and correlations that may be indicative of underlying problems.

Example prompt:

```
"Analyze the past year's sales data and identify any
patterns or trends that may be contributing to our recent
decline in sales."
```

Detecting patterns and anomalies

AI can detect patterns and anomalies in data that may be difficult or time-consuming for humans to identify. This can help leaders uncover potential issues before they escalate into bigger problems.

Example prompt:

```
"Review our customer support tickets from the last three
months and identify any recurring issues or unusual patterns
that may suggest underlying problems with our product or
service."
```

Uncovering hidden relationships

AI can help leaders uncover hidden relationships between variables that may be contributing to a problem. By understanding these relationships, leaders can develop targeted solutions to address the root cause.

Example prompt:

```
"Analyze the relationship between our product return rate
and factors such as product quality, shipping time, and
customer service, to identify the main drivers behind the
high return rate."
```

Categorizing and prioritizing problems

AI can help leaders categorize and prioritize problems based on factors such as urgency, impact, and resource requirements. This can enable leaders to focus their efforts on the most critical issues and allocate resources effectively.

Example prompt:

"Based on our analysis of customer complaints, categorize
and prioritize the identified issues according to their
impact on customer satisfaction and the resources required
to address them."

Generating hypotheses

AI can help leaders generate hypotheses about the root causes of a problem by considering different factors and exploring various scenarios. These hypotheses can then be tested and validated to determine the most likely cause of the problem.

Example prompt:

"Generate a list of possible root causes for the decline in
our employee engagement and suggest ways to test and
validate each hypothesis."

Predictive analytics

AI can help leaders predict potential problems before they occur by analyzing historical data and identifying patterns that may lead to future issues. This can enable leaders to proactively address potential problems and minimize their impact.

Example prompt:

```
"Based on historical data, predict any potential issues that
may arise with our supply chain in the next six months and
suggest ways to mitigate these risks."
```

By utilizing AI tools like ChatGPT and GPT-4 in root cause analysis and problem identification, leaders can gain deeper insights into the underlying issues, prioritize their efforts effectively, and develop targeted solutions. This can ultimately contribute to more effective problem-solving and improved organizational performance. In the following subchapters, we will continue to explore AI-assisted problem-solving and provide additional practical examples and prompt templates to help leaders harness the power of AI.

6.5 AI for Developing and Evaluating Solutions

Developing and evaluating solutions is a critical aspect of problem-solving for leaders. AI can assist in this process by generating ideas, evaluating the feasibility of different solutions, and simulating potential outcomes. In this subchapter, we will discuss various ways AI can help leaders in developing and evaluating solutions, and provide Example prompts to demonstrate their application.

Generating solution ideas

AI can help leaders generate solution ideas by considering a wide range of possibilities and drawing upon its extensive knowledge base.

Example prompt:

"Generate a list of possible solutions to address the issue
of high employee turnover in our organization."

Evaluating feasibility

AI can help leaders evaluate the feasibility of different solutions by considering factors such as resource requirements, cost, and potential impact.

Example prompt:

"Assess the feasibility of implementing a remote work policy
to improve employee satisfaction and retention. Consider
factors such as cost, productivity, and the impact on team
collaboration."

Simulating potential outcomes

AI can help leaders simulate potential outcomes of various solutions, allowing them to make more informed decisions and anticipate potential risks.

Example prompt:

"Simulate the potential outcomes of implementing a flexible
work schedule for our employees, including the potential
impact on productivity, employee satisfaction, and
operational efficiency."

Analyzing risks and trade-offs

AI can help leaders analyze the risks and trade-offs associated with different solutions, enabling them to make better-informed decisions and minimize potential negative consequences.

Example prompt:

"Analyze the risks and trade-offs of outsourcing our customer support services to a third-party provider, considering factors such as cost, customer satisfaction, and quality control."

Optimizing solutions

AI can help leaders optimize solutions by identifying areas for improvement and suggesting modifications that can enhance effectiveness and efficiency.

Example prompt:

"Optimize our proposed customer retention strategy by identifying areas for improvement and suggesting changes that could enhance its effectiveness and efficiency."

Monitoring progress and refining solutions

AI can help leaders monitor the progress of implemented solutions and refine them as needed, based on real-time feedback and data analysis.

Example prompt:

"Monitor the progress of our new employee training program and suggest refinements based on feedback and performance

```
metrics."
```

By leveraging AI tools like ChatGPT and GPT-4 in developing and evaluating solutions, leaders can enhance their problem-solving capabilities, make more informed decisions, and drive better outcomes for their organizations. In the subsequent subchapters, we will continue to explore AI-assisted problem-solving and provide practical examples and prompt templates to help leaders effectively harness the power of AI.

6.6 AI for Continuous Improvement and Innovation

Continuous improvement and innovation are essential for leaders to ensure their organizations remain competitive and adaptive in today's rapidly changing business landscape. AI can play a vital role in facilitating continuous improvement and fostering a culture of innovation. In this subchapter, we will discuss various ways AI can support leaders in this endeavor and provide Example prompts to demonstrate their application.

Identifying areas for improvement

AI can help leaders identify areas for improvement within their organizations by analyzing performance data, benchmarking against industry standards, and detecting patterns or anomalies.

Example prompt:

"Analyze our organization's performance data over the past year and identify areas where we can improve our efficiency and effectiveness."

Benchmarking against industry standards

AI can help leaders benchmark their organization's performance against industry standards and best practices, allowing them to identify gaps and areas for improvement.

Example prompt:

"Compare our customer satisfaction metrics with industry benchmarks and identify areas where we can improve our customer experience."

Fostering a culture of innovation

AI can help leaders foster a culture of innovation within their organizations by generating new ideas, identifying opportunities for innovation, and encouraging open communication and collaboration.

Example prompt:

"Generate a list of potential innovative projects or initiatives that could help our organization improve its competitiveness and market position."

Encouraging open communication and collaboration

AI can help leaders encourage open communication and collaboration within their teams by providing insights, facilitating discussions, and supporting decision-making.

Example prompt:

"Provide a list of discussion questions or topics that can
be used in our next team meeting to encourage open
communication and collaboration around innovation and
continuous improvement."

Evaluating the impact of implemented improvements

AI can help leaders evaluate the impact of implemented improvements by monitoring progress, measuring outcomes, and analyzing the effectiveness of the changes.

Example prompt:

"Monitor the progress of our newly implemented process
improvement initiative and analyze its impact on efficiency,
productivity, and customer satisfaction."

Adapting to change and learning from failures

AI can help leaders adapt to change and learn from failures by analyzing data, identifying patterns, and providing insights into the root causes of unsuccessful initiatives.

Example prompt:

```
"Analyze the reasons behind the failure of our recent
product launch and provide recommendations for how we can
learn from this experience and improve our future product
development efforts."
```

By incorporating AI tools like ChatGPT and GPT-4 into their contin-uous improvement and innovation efforts, leaders can gain valuable insights, make more informed decisions, and drive positive change within their organizations. In the following subchapters, we will con-tinue to explore AI-assisted problem-solving and provide additional practical examples and prompt templates to help leaders harness the power of AI.

6.7 Collaborating with AI for Multi-disciplinary Problem Solving

Multi-disciplinary problem-solving is essential for leaders, as complex challenges often require input and collaboration from different areas of expertise. AI can be an invaluable resource in this process, enabling leaders to access a wide range of knowledge and insights, and facilitating collaboration across diverse disciplines. In this subchapter, we will discuss various ways AI can support leaders in multi-disciplinary problem-solving and provide Example prompts to demonstrate their application.

Accessing diverse knowledge and expertise

AI can help leaders access diverse knowledge and expertise by drawing upon its extensive knowledge base, which spans various domains and disciplines.

Example prompt:

"Provide an overview of the key factors affecting supply
chain management in the pharmaceutical industry and suggest
potential strategies for improvement."

Connecting experts and facilitating collaboration

AI can help leaders connect experts from different disciplines and facilitate collaboration by identifying relevant stakeholders and encouraging open communication.

Example prompt:

"Identify a list of experts in our organization who can
contribute to a multi-disciplinary task force focused on
improving our product development process."

Generating cross-disciplinary insights

AI can help leaders generate cross-disciplinary insights by synthesizing information and perspectives from different fields and providing a holistic view of the problem at hand.

Example prompt:

"Analyze the impact of our organization's digital
transformation on both our marketing and supply chain

strategies, and provide recommendations for aligning these efforts."

Supporting decision-making in complex environments

AI can help leaders make informed decisions in complex environments by providing comprehensive analyses, identifying potential risks and trade-offs, and simulating potential outcomes.

Example prompt:

"Evaluate the potential impact of adopting a circular economy model on our organization's financial performance, environmental sustainability, and social responsibility."

Encouraging creative problem-solving

AI can help leaders encourage creative problem-solving by generating novel ideas, identifying unconventional solutions, and inspiring out-of-the-box thinking.

Example prompt:

"Generate a list of unconventional marketing strategies that could help our organization stand out in a crowded market and attract new customers."

By leveraging AI tools like ChatGPT and GPT-4 in multi-disciplinary problem-solving, leaders can access diverse knowledge and expertise, foster collaboration across disciplines, and make more informed decisions to address complex challenges. In the subsequent subchapters,

we will continue to explore AI-assisted problem-solving and provide
practical examples and prompt templates to help leaders effectively
harness the power of AI.

6.8 Prompt Templates for Problem-solving Situations

In this subchapter, we provide prompt templates designed to assist
leaders in various problem-solving situations. These templates can
be adapted to address specific challenges and help leaders effectively
harness the power of AI to find solutions.

Identifying the root cause of a problem

```
"Analyze the data related to [problem] and identify the root
cause(s) along with contributing factors."
```

This prompt template helps leaders identify the root cause of a specific
problem by analyzing relevant data and considering contributing
factors.

Generating potential solutions

```
"Generate a list of potential solutions to address the issue
of [problem] considering both short-term and long-term
strategies."
```

This prompt template encourages the generation of potential solutions for a specific problem, considering various perspectives and
approaches.

Evaluating the pros and cons of different solutions

> "Compare the pros and cons of the following solutions for
> [problem]: [Solution A], [Solution B], and [Solution C],
> considering factors such as feasibility, cost, impact, and
> risks."

This prompt template supports leaders in evaluating the pros and cons of different solutions, considering factors such as feasibility, cost, impact, and risks.

Prioritizing solutions based on specific criteria

> "Rank the following solutions for [problem] based on
> criteria such as urgency, potential impact, and resource
> requirements: [Solution A], [Solution B], and [Solution C]."

This prompt template helps leaders prioritize solutions based on specific criteria such as urgency, potential impact, and resource requirements.

Developing an action plan to implement a chosen solution

> "Develop an action plan to implement [chosen solution] for
> [problem], including necessary steps, resources, and
> timelines."

This prompt template assists leaders in developing an action plan to implement a chosen solution, outlining necessary steps, resources, and timelines.

Monitoring progress and evaluating the effectiveness of imple-

mented solutions

"Monitor the progress of [implemented solution] for
[problem] and evaluate its effectiveness in addressing the
issue, considering key performance indicators and any
unexpected outcomes."

This prompt template supports leaders in monitoring the progress of
implemented solutions and evaluating their effectiveness in addressing
the problem at hand.

Learning from failures and adapting to change

"Analyze the reasons behind the failure of [unsuccessful
initiative] and provide recommendations for how we can learn
from this experience and improve our approach to [problem]
in the future."

This prompt template helps leaders learn from failures, adapt to
change, and refine their problem-solving strategies.

Identifying potential risks and challenges

"Identify potential risks and challenges associated with
implementing [solution or initiative] and suggest strategies
to mitigate or overcome them."

This prompt template helps leaders identify potential risks and
challenges associated with a specific solution or initiative.

Assessing the impact of external factors on a problem

```
"Assess the impact of external factors, including market
trends, technological advancements, and regulatory changes,
on the issue of [problem]."
```

This prompt template assists leaders in assessing the impact of external factors, such as market trends, technological advancements, or regulatory changes, on a specific problem.

Gathering feedback from stakeholders

```
"Collect feedback from stakeholders, including employees,
customers, and suppliers, on the issue of [problem] and
suggest ways to address their concerns."
```

This prompt template supports leaders in gathering feedback from various stakeholders to better understand a problem and consider diverse perspectives.

Applying lessons learned from past experiences

```
"Review past experiences related to [similar problem or
situation] and identify lessons learned that could be
applied to the current issue of [problem]."
```

This prompt template helps leaders apply lessons learned from past experiences to current problem-solving situations.

Facilitating brainstorming sessions with team members

"Generate a list of discussion questions and topics to
facilitate a brainstorming session with team members on the
issue of [problem]."

This prompt template assists leaders in facilitating brainstorming sessions with team members to generate innovative ideas and solutions.

Seeking expert advice and opinions

"Identify relevant experts in the field of [problem's
domain] and provide a list of questions to ask them for
their insights on [problem] and potential solutions."

This prompt template supports leaders in seeking expert advice and opinions to better understand a problem and evaluate potential solutions.

Analyzing the potential long-term consequences of a solution

"Analyze the potential long-term consequences of
implementing [solution] for [problem], considering factors
such as sustainability, scalability, and impact on
stakeholders."

This prompt template helps leaders analyze the potential long-term consequences of a solution, considering factors such as sustainability, scalability, and impact on stakeholders.

Evaluating the ethical implications of a solution

```
"Evaluate the ethical implications of implementing
[solution] for [problem], considering factors such as
fairness, transparency, and potential harm."
```

This prompt template assists leaders in evaluating the ethical implications of a specific solution, considering factors such as fairness, transparency, and potential harm.

Identifying opportunities for improvement and innovation

```
"Identify opportunities for improvement and innovation
within our organization or industry, focusing on areas such
as process optimization, product development, and customer
experience."
```

This prompt template supports leaders in identifying opportunities for improvement and innovation within their organization or industry.

Building consensus and buy-in for a solution

```
"Develop a strategy to build consensus and buy-in for
[solution] among team members and other stakeholders,
including effective communication techniques and addressing
potential concerns."
```

This prompt template helps leaders build consensus and buy-in for a specific solution among team members and other stakeholders

These prompt templates can be customized to fit a wide range of problem-solving situations, helping leaders make informed decisions and effectively tackle complex challenges with the assistance of AI tools like ChatGPT and GPT-4.

7

Collaboration and Delegation with AI

In Chapter 7, we will explore the crucial role AI can play in enhancing collaboration and delegation within an organization. As leaders strive to create synergistic environments and delegate tasks effectively, AI can serve as a valuable tool in streamlining these processes. This chapter will provide insights into various aspects of AI-assisted collaboration and delegation through the following subchapters:

1. **Facilitating Collaborative Brainstorming Sessions:** This subchapter will discuss how AI can be used to facilitate brainstorming sessions, encouraging innovative ideas and fostering a collaborative atmosphere.

2. **AI-assisted Delegation:** In this section, we will examine how AI can assist leaders in delegating tasks to team members based on their skills, availability, and other relevant factors, ensuring efficient task distribution.

3. **Streamlining Cross-Functional Collaboration with AI:** We will explore how AI can help streamline cross-functional collaboration, breaking down barriers between departments and

promoting cohesive teamwork.

4. **AI in Task Automation and Delegation:** This subchapter will focus on the role of AI in automating and delegating tasks, freeing up time and resources for leaders to concentrate on strategic decision-making.

5. **Maintaining Accountability and Oversight with AI:** In this section, we will discuss how AI can help leaders maintain accountability and oversight, ensuring tasks are completed on time and to the required standards.

6. **Fostering Collaboration between Humans and AI:** We will delve into the ways in which leaders can encourage cooperation between human team members and AI, creating a harmonious and effective working environment.

7. **Developing Delegation Strategies with AI Assistance:** This subchapter will examine how AI can aid in the development of delegation strategies, optimizing task allocation and ensuring the most efficient use of resources.

8. **Prompt Templates for Delegation and Collaboration:** In this section, we will provide prompt templates designed to facilitate AI-assisted delegation and collaboration, empowering leaders to harness the potential of AI in managing their teams effectively.

Throughout this chapter, our goal is to provide a comprehensive understanding of how AI can be utilized to enhance collaboration and delegation within an organization. By integrating AI into their leadership toolkit, leaders can create more efficient and harmonious working environments that drive success and growth.

7.1 Facilitating Collaborative Brainstorming Sessions

The power of collaboration is undeniable, and brainstorming sessions are one of the most effective ways to generate ideas and find innovative solutions. AI tools like ChatGPT and GPT-4 can be invaluable assets in facilitating collaborative brainstorming sessions, providing leaders with useful insights, idea starters, and discussion prompts.

Benefits of AI-assisted brainstorming:

1. **Idea generation:** AI can quickly generate a wide range of ideas based on a given topic or problem, helping to jump-start the brainstorming process.

2. **Diverse perspectives:** AI can analyze large amounts of data from various sources, ensuring that ideas and insights from different perspectives are considered during the brainstorming session.

3. **Reducing bias:** AI can help reduce personal biases and group-think by providing objective insights and analysis.

4. **Encouraging participation:** AI-generated prompts can encourage team members to contribute their ideas and engage in the discussion.

5. **Time efficiency:** AI can help streamline the brainstorming process by providing well-structured prompts and targeted insights, saving time and keeping the discussion focused.

Example prompts for AI-assisted brainstorming sessions:

"Generate a list of innovative ideas to improve [product or service] based on current customer feedback and industry trends."

"Identify potential collaboration opportunities between the marketing and engineering departments to enhance the customer experience."

"Provide a list of discussion topics to facilitate a brainstorming session on developing more sustainable business practices."

"Suggest potential solutions for addressing the challenges of remote work and fostering effective communication within the team."

"Analyze competitor strategies and identify areas where our organization can differentiate itself in the market."

By using AI tools like ChatGPT and GPT-4 in brainstorming sessions, leaders can foster an environment that encourages creativity and innovation, helping their teams to develop unique solutions to complex problems. The AI-generated prompts and insights can inspire team members to think beyond their usual perspectives, making brainstorming sessions more engaging and productive.

7.2 AI-assisted Delegation

Effective delegation is a critical skill for leaders, as it enables them to allocate tasks and responsibilities to the right team members, ensuring that projects are completed efficiently and successfully. AI tools like ChatGPT and GPT-4 can provide valuable assistance in the delegation process, helping leaders make more informed decisions based on data and insights.

Benefits of AI-assisted delegation:

1. **Skill matching:** AI can analyze the skills, experience, and strengths of team members to identify the best candidates for specific tasks or projects.

2. **Workload balancing:** AI can assess the current workload of team members, helping leaders distribute tasks more evenly and avoid overloading any individual.

3. **Performance monitoring:** AI can track the performance of team members over time, providing insights into their strengths and areas for improvement, which can inform future delegation decisions.

4. **Continuous learning:** AI can identify skills gaps within the team and suggest relevant training or development opportunities to address these gaps, ensuring team members continue to grow and excel in their roles.

5. **Time-saving:** AI can streamline the delegation process by providing targeted insights and recommendations, freeing up leaders to focus on other strategic priorities.

Example prompts for AI-assisted delegation:

"Analyze the skills and experience of my team members and recommend the best candidates for leading our upcoming product launch."

"Assess the current workload of each team member and suggest a balanced distribution of tasks for our upcoming project."

"Identify areas for improvement within the team and recommend relevant training or development opportunities."

"Provide a summary of each team member's performance in the last quarter, highlighting their strengths and achievements."

"Generate a list of tasks that can be delegated to team members with lower workloads to improve overall team efficiency."

By leveraging AI tools like ChatGPT and GPT-4 for delegation, leaders can make more informed decisions about task allocation, ensuring that team members are engaged, challenged, and working to their strengths. This not only improves the overall efficiency and effectiveness of the team but also fosters a positive work environment in which team members feel supported and valued.

7.3 Streamlining Cross-Functional Collaboration with AI

Cross-functional collaboration is essential for organizations that want to break down silos, improve communication, and drive innovation. AI tools like ChatGPT and GPT-4 can significantly enhance cross-functional collaboration by providing valuable insights, facilitating communication, and identifying areas for improvement.

Benefits of AI-assisted cross-functional collaboration:

1. **Enhanced communication:** AI can help facilitate communication between different departments by providing relevant information, insights, and discussion prompts tailored to each function's specific needs and priorities.

2. **Resource optimization:** AI can analyze the skills and expertise of team members from various departments, helping leaders to identify the best candidates for cross-functional collaboration and ensuring the efficient use of resources.

3. **Improved decision-making:** AI can provide insights and analysis from diverse perspectives, allowing cross-functional teams to make more informed decisions that consider the needs and priorities of multiple stakeholders.

4. **Conflict resolution:** AI can help identify potential areas of conflict or disagreement between departments and suggest strategies for resolving these issues, fostering a more collaborative and harmonious work environment.

5. **Innovation and creativity:** AI can support cross-functional teams in generating innovative ideas and solutions by providing diverse insights and perspectives based on large amounts of data and information.

Example prompts for AI-assisted cross-functional collaboration:

"Generate a list of potential collaboration opportunities between the marketing and product development teams that could drive innovation and growth."

"Analyze the skills and expertise of team members from different departments and recommend the best candidates for a cross-functional project team."

"Provide a summary of the key priorities and concerns of each department involved in an upcoming project, to facilitate better communication and understanding between teams."

"Identify potential areas of conflict between the sales and engineering departments and suggest strategies for resolving these issues."

"Suggest discussion topics and activities for a
cross-functional workshop aimed at fostering collaboration
and innovation."

By integrating AI tools like ChatGPT and GPT-4 into cross-functional collaboration processes, organizations can break down barriers between departments, improve communication, and foster a more innovative and agile work environment. These AI-driven insights and strategies can help leaders manage their teams more effectively, ensure the efficient use of resources, and drive greater success in their cross-functional projects.

7.4 AI in Task Automation and Delegation

In addition to providing valuable insights and decision-making support, AI tools like ChatGPT and GPT-4 can also help automate and delegate various tasks, freeing up leaders to focus on more strategic priorities. This can significantly improve team efficiency and productivity, while also empowering team members to take on greater responsibility and ownership of their work.

Benefits of AI-assisted task automation and delegation:

1. **Increased efficiency:** By automating routine tasks and processes, AI can help teams complete their work more quickly and efficiently, resulting in greater overall productivity.
2. **Enhanced accuracy:** AI tools can reduce the likelihood of human error in tasks such as data entry and analysis, leading to more

accurate and reliable results.

3. **Time-saving:** By delegating tasks to AI, leaders can free up more time to focus on strategic priorities and decision-making, rather than getting bogged down in routine tasks.

4. **Employee development:** AI can help identify tasks that can be delegated to team members, allowing them to develop their skills and take on greater responsibility within the team.

5. **Scalability:** AI tools can be easily scaled to handle larger volumes of work or new tasks as the organization grows, ensuring continued efficiency and productivity.

Example prompts for AI-assisted task automation and delegation:

```
"Identify routine tasks within our team's responsibilities
that could be automated using AI tools."
```

```
"Suggest ways in which AI can improve the accuracy and
efficiency of our data analysis processes."
```

```
"Analyze my current workload and recommend tasks that could
be delegated to AI or team members to free up more time for
strategic decision-making."
```

```
"Evaluate the skills and capabilities of team members and
suggest tasks that could be delegated to them for
development purposes."
```

```
"Provide a plan for scaling our AI tools to handle increased
workloads and new tasks as the organization grows."
```

By embracing AI-assisted task automation and delegation, leaders can create more efficient and productive teams, allowing them to focus on higher-level strategic priorities. This not only improves the overall performance of the team but also creates a more supportive and empowering work environment in which team members can continue to learn, grow, and take on new challenges.

7.5 Maintaining Accountability and Oversight with AI

As AI becomes more integrated into various aspects of leadership roles, it's essential to ensure that accountability and oversight are maintained. While AI can help automate tasks and streamline processes, leaders must still provide guidance, direction, and supervision to ensure that the work aligns with the organization's goals and values.

Benefits of maintaining accountability and oversight with AI:

1. **Alignment with organizational goals:** By providing oversight, leaders can ensure that AI-driven processes and decision-making are consistent with the organization's strategic objectives and values.

2. **Ethical considerations:** Leaders can monitor and guide AI tools to ensure that they operate ethically, avoiding potential biases or inappropriate actions that could harm the organization's reputation or stakeholder relationships.

3. **Trust and transparency:** By maintaining accountability and oversight, leaders can foster trust and transparency within their teams and with external stakeholders, demonstrating that AI tools are being used responsibly and effectively.

4. **Continuous improvement:** Oversight allows leaders to identify areas where AI tools and processes can be improved, ensuring that the organization continues to evolve and adapt to changing circumstances and technologies.

5. **Employee engagement:** By maintaining a balance between AI-driven automation and human decision-making, leaders can ensure that team members remain engaged and invested in their work, promoting a positive and collaborative work environment.

Example prompts for maintaining accountability and oversight with AI:

```
"Provide a set of guidelines and best practices for our team
to follow when using AI tools, ensuring alignment with
organizational goals and ethical considerations."
```

```
"Suggest metrics and indicators that we can track to monitor
the effectiveness and ethical use of AI tools within our
```

team."

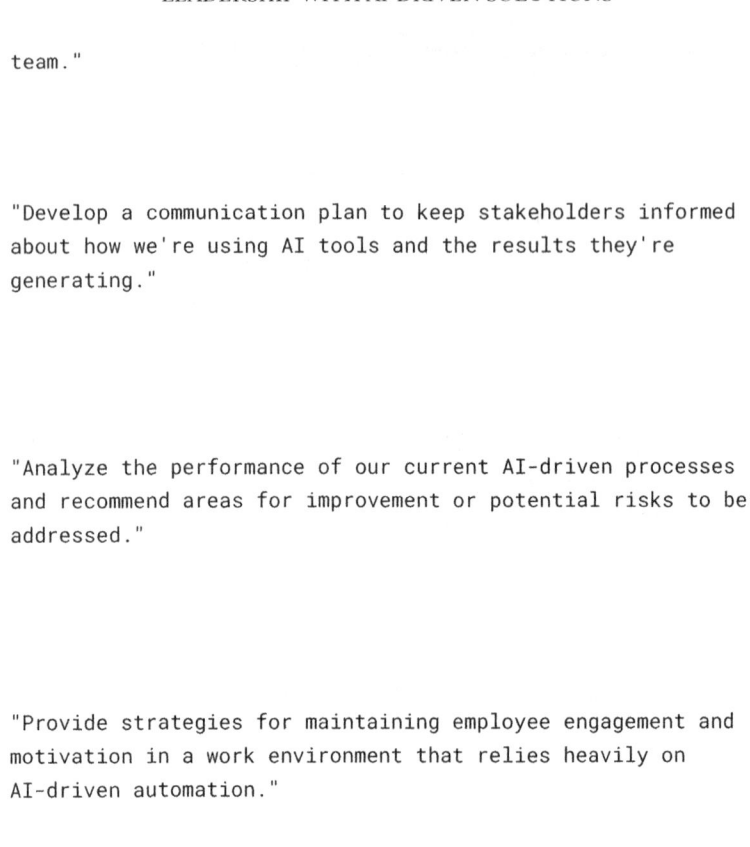

"Develop a communication plan to keep stakeholders informed
about how we're using AI tools and the results they're
generating."

"Analyze the performance of our current AI-driven processes
and recommend areas for improvement or potential risks to be
addressed."

"Provide strategies for maintaining employee engagement and
motivation in a work environment that relies heavily on
AI-driven automation."

By maintaining accountability and oversight over AI-driven processes, leaders can ensure that their teams remain focused on the organization's strategic objectives and values. This approach promotes trust, transparency, and continuous improvement, creating a more resilient and adaptable organization that can successfully navigate the challenges and opportunities presented by emerging technologies.

7.6 Fostering Collaboration between Humans and AI

As AI tools become more integrated into leadership roles, fostering collaboration between humans and AI becomes increasingly important. This collaboration can lead to more effective decision-making, increased productivity, and a stronger, more unified team.

Benefits of fostering human-AI collaboration:

1. **Enhanced decision-making:** Combining human intuition and experience with AI-driven insights and analysis can lead to more well-rounded and informed decisions.
2. **Increased productivity:** By leveraging the strengths of both humans and AI, teams can work more efficiently, completing tasks faster and with greater accuracy.
3. **Balanced perspectives:** AI can provide unbiased, data-driven insights that complement human judgment, resulting in a more balanced approach to problem-solving and decision-making.
4. **Improved learning and adaptation:** By working closely with AI tools, team members can learn from the AI's insights and analysis, while the AI can learn from human interactions and feedback, leading to continuous improvement and adaptation.
5. **Creativity and innovation:** Combining human creativity with AI-driven insights can lead to novel ideas and innovative solutions that may not have been possible with either humans or AI working alone.

Example prompts for fostering human-AI collaboration:

"Identify the strengths and weaknesses of both humans and AI
in our team's decision-making process and suggest ways to
leverage these strengths for better results."

"Develop a plan to integrate AI tools more closely with our
team's workflow, ensuring that team members understand how
to collaborate effectively with AI."

"Analyze our current decision-making process and provide
recommendations for incorporating AI-driven insights to
achieve a more balanced approach."

"Suggest training and development initiatives to help our
team members better understand and work with AI tools."

"Propose strategies for promoting creativity and innovation
within our team by combining human and AI-driven insights."

By fostering collaboration between humans and AI, leaders can create
a more dynamic and effective team that leverages the strengths of both
to achieve better results. This approach not only improves decision-
making and productivity but also promotes learning, adaptation, and

innovation within the team, ensuring ongoing growth and success in an increasingly AI-driven world.

7.7 Developing Delegation Strategies with AI Assistance

Delegation is a critical leadership skill, and AI can be a valuable tool in helping leaders delegate tasks more effectively. By leveraging AI to analyze team members' skills, strengths, and weaknesses, as well as the specific requirements of tasks, leaders can make more informed decisions about how to distribute work across their teams.

Benefits of developing delegation strategies with AI assistance:

1. **Efficient task allocation:** AI can help leaders identify which team members are best suited for specific tasks, ensuring that work is distributed efficiently and effectively.
2. **Skill development:** By delegating tasks based on team members' strengths and areas for growth, leaders can help their team members develop new skills and improve existing ones.
3. **Increased productivity:** Effective delegation can lead to higher productivity, as team members are given tasks that align with their strengths and interests.
4. **Greater trust and autonomy:** Delegating tasks to team members based on their skills and abilities demonstrates trust in their capabilities, fostering a sense of autonomy and ownership over their work.
5. **Workload management:** Using AI to analyze team members' workloads can help leaders ensure that tasks are distributed evenly, avoiding burnout and maintaining overall team morale.

Example prompts for developing delegation strategies with
AI assistance:

"Analyze the skills and strengths of our team members and
recommend appropriate tasks for each individual based on
their abilities."

"Identify areas for growth and skill development within our
team, and suggest tasks that can help team members improve
in these areas."

"Review the workload distribution among our team members and
recommend strategies for balancing workloads more
effectively."

"Provide guidelines for fostering trust and autonomy within
our team through effective delegation practices."

"Assess the impact of our current delegation practices on
team productivity and morale, and provide recommendations

for improvement."

By incorporating AI assistance into their delegation strategies, leaders can make more informed decisions about task allocation, skill development, and workload management. This approach not only increases team productivity but also fosters trust, autonomy, and overall team morale, contributing to a more engaged and effective workforce.

7.8 Prompt templates for delegation and collaboration

Here are some prompt templates designed to help leaders delegate tasks and foster collaboration with the help of AI.

Identifying suitable tasks for team members

```
"Analyze the skills, strengths, and weaknesses of {team
member's name} and recommend tasks suitable for their
abilities."
```

Use this prompt to analyze team members' skills, strengths, and weaknesses and identify suitable tasks for each individual.

Assessing team collaboration

```
"Assess the current collaboration level within our team and
provide recommendations to enhance collaboration among team
members."
```

This prompt helps evaluate the current level of collaboration within the team and suggests ways to improve it.

Delegating tasks for skill development

> "Identify tasks that can help {team member's name} develop
> new skills or improve their current skills in {specific
> area}."

Use this prompt to identify tasks that can help team members develop new skills or improve existing ones.

Balancing workload among team members

> "Analyze the current workload distribution among our team
> members and recommend strategies to balance workloads more
> effectively."

This prompt helps analyze workload distribution within the team and suggests strategies to balance workloads more effectively.

Fostering trust and autonomy through delegation

> "Develop strategies to promote trust and autonomy within our
> team by delegating tasks based on team members' skills and
> abilities."

Use this prompt to develop strategies that foster trust and autonomy among team members through effective delegation practices.

Improving team productivity through delegation

```
"Evaluate the impact of our current delegation practices on
team productivity and provide recommendations for
improvement."
```

This prompt helps assess the impact of current delegation practices on team productivity and suggests improvements.

Promoting collaboration between humans and AI

```
"Develop a plan to integrate AI tools into our team's
workflow and foster effective collaboration between humans
and AI."
```

Use this prompt to develop a plan for integrating AI tools into the team's workflow and promoting effective collaboration between humans and AI.

AI-assisted decision-making in delegation

```
"Provide AI-driven insights to inform my decision on which
tasks to delegate to {team member's name}."
```

This prompt helps leaders make informed decisions about delegating tasks using AI-driven insights.

Identifying collaboration opportunities

```
"Analyze the skills and interests of our team members and
suggest potential collaboration opportunities between them."
```

Use this prompt to identify potential collaboration opportunities among team members based on their skills and interests.

Delegating long-term projects

> "Identify the best-suited team members to work on a
> long-term project related to {project topic}, considering
> their skills, experience, and availability."

This prompt helps determine the most suitable team members for long-term projects based on their skills, experience, and availability.

Facilitating effective team communication

> "Provide recommendations for improving team communication to
> enhance collaboration and productivity."

Use this prompt to gather insights on how to improve communication within the team for better collaboration.

Monitoring delegated tasks

> "Track the progress of the tasks delegated to {team member's
> name} and identify any potential issues or bottlenecks that
> need to be addressed."

This prompt helps leaders track the progress of delegated tasks and identify any potential issues or bottlenecks.

Encouraging cross-functional collaboration

```
"Identify opportunities for cross-functional collaboration
between our team and other teams within the organization."
```

Use this prompt to identify opportunities for collaboration between different departments or teams within the organization.

Assigning tasks based on team members' preferences

```
"Analyze the preferences of {team member's name} and suggest
tasks that align with their interests and passions."
```

This prompt helps leaders delegate tasks according to team members' preferences, leading to higher engagement and job satisfaction.

Overcoming collaboration challenges

```
"Identify challenges that are hindering effective
collaboration within our team and suggest strategies to
overcome them."
```

Use this prompt to identify challenges affecting team collaboration and propose solutions to overcome them.

Developing a collaborative culture

```
"Develop a plan to create a collaborative culture within our
team, fostering open communication and shared
problem-solving."
```

This prompt helps leaders develop a plan to create a culture of collaboration within the team.

Matching tasks to team members' learning goals

"Identify tasks that align with the learning goals of {team
member's name} and support their personal growth and
development."

Use this prompt to delegate tasks that align with team members' learning goals, promoting personal growth and development.

Encouraging knowledge sharing

"Create a plan to encourage knowledge sharing within our
team, supporting collaboration and collective learning."

This prompt helps leaders create a plan for promoting knowledge sharing within the team, fostering collaboration and collective learning.

Evaluating team collaboration tools

"Evaluate the effectiveness of the collaboration tools
currently used by our team and recommend potential
improvements or alternative tools."

Use this prompt to assess the effectiveness of the collaboration tools currently used by the team and identify potential improvements or alternatives.

Assessing team members' readiness for delegation

```
"Assess the readiness of {team member's name} for additional
responsibility and delegation, considering their skills,
workload, and performance."
```

This prompt helps leaders determine if a team member is ready for additional responsibility through delegation.

Feel free to customize these prompt templates to better suit your specific needs and context. By using these templates, you can leverage AI to improve your delegation and collaboration practices, ultimately leading to a more productive and engaged team.

8

Financial Management and AI

I n Chapter 8, we will delve into the world of financial management and explore how AI can assist in various financial tasks and processes. As organizations strive to make data-driven decisions and maintain financial stability, AI can be a powerful tool in making more informed and strategic choices. This chapter will cover a range of subchapters to provide a comprehensive understanding of AI's role in financial management:

1. **Budgeting and Forecasting with AI:** This subchapter will discuss how AI can help organizations create more accurate budgets and financial forecasts by analyzing historical data, current trends, and other relevant factors.

2. **Financial Analysis and Insights:** In this section, we will examine the role of AI in providing valuable financial insights and analysis, enabling leaders to make informed decisions based on real-time data.

3. **Risk Management and Compliance with AI:** We will explore how AI can support organizations in risk management and compliance efforts, helping to identify potential threats and

ensuring adherence to regulations.

4. **AI for Cash Flow Management:** This subchapter will delve into how AI can assist in cash flow management, helping organizations optimize their working capital and maintain financial stability.

5. **AI in Investment Decision-Making:** In this section, we will discuss how AI can support investment decision-making by providing insights on market trends, potential risks, and opportunities.

6. **AI for Financial Performance Monitoring:** We will explore how AI can help organizations monitor their financial performance and provide timely alerts for potential issues, enabling proactive decision-making.

7. **AI for Fraud Detection and Prevention:** This subchapter will examine how AI can be used to detect and prevent fraudulent activities, safeguarding organizations' financial assets and reputation.

8. **Prompt Templates for Financial Management Scenarios:** In this section, we will provide prompt templates designed to facilitate AI-assisted financial management, empowering leaders to harness the potential of AI in managing their organization's finances effectively.

Throughout this chapter, our aim is to offer a thorough understanding of the ways AI can be utilized to enhance financial management within organizations. By integrating AI into their financial strategies, leaders can make more informed decisions, optimize financial performance, and mitigate risks, ultimately driving growth and success.

8.1 Budgeting and Forecasting with AI

In today's dynamic business environment, accurate budgeting and forecasting are essential for making informed financial decisions and ensuring an organization's long-term success. AI technologies like GPT-4 can play a crucial role in enhancing the accuracy and efficiency of these processes. In this subchapter, we will explore how AI can be employed to create better budgets and forecasts.

Benefits of using AI for budgeting and forecasting:

1. **Improved accuracy:** AI can analyze large amounts of historical data and identify patterns and trends, which can lead to more accurate predictions and better-informed budgeting decisions.

2. **Time and resource efficiency:** AI can automate and streamline the budgeting and forecasting process, reducing the time and effort required from the finance team and allowing them to focus on other strategic tasks.

3. **Enhanced scenario planning:** AI can help leaders explore different scenarios and their potential financial implications, enabling them to make better decisions under uncertainty.

4. **Real-time updates and adjustments:** AI can continuously monitor financial data and provide real-time updates and adjustments to budgets and forecasts, ensuring that they remain relevant and accurate.

Example prompts for using AI in budgeting and forecasting:

"Analyze historical revenue data for the past five years and predict the revenue growth for the next year."

"Identify the key drivers of revenue growth in our industry and suggest strategies to capitalize on these trends."

"Based on our current expenses and planned initiatives, estimate our operating expenses for the next fiscal year."

"Evaluate the financial impact of various business scenarios, such as market expansions or product launches, on our budget and forecasts."

"Monitor our financial performance in real-time and suggest adjustments to our budget and forecasts as needed."

By leveraging AI technologies like GPT-4, leaders can create more accurate budgets and forecasts, enabling them to make better financial decisions, allocate resources more effectively, and ensure the long-term success of their organization.

8.2 Financial Analysis and Insights

Financial analysis is critical for understanding an organization's financial health and making informed decisions. AI technologies like GPT-4 can significantly enhance the financial analysis process by providing deep insights and identifying patterns and trends that might not be apparent through manual analysis. In this subchapter, we will discuss how AI can be utilized to improve financial analysis and offer valuable insights to leaders.

Benefits of using AI for financial analysis:

1. **Data-driven insights:** AI can analyze vast amounts of financial data quickly and accurately, providing leaders with data-driven insights to support their decision-making process.
2. **Identifying trends and patterns:** AI can uncover hidden patterns and trends in financial data, helping leaders understand the underlying factors driving their organization's financial performance.
3. **Enhanced predictive capabilities:** AI can predict future financial performance based on historical data and current market conditions, allowing leaders to plan and strategize more effectively.
4. **Improved efficiency:** AI can automate various aspects of financial analysis, reducing the time and effort required from the finance team and allowing them to focus on other strategic tasks.

Example prompts for using AI in financial analysis:

"Analyze our financial statements and identify the key financial ratios to assess our organization's financial health."

"Compare our financial performance with industry benchmarks and identify areas where we excel or need improvement."

"Identify trends and patterns in our revenue and expenses over the past three years and suggest possible explanations for these trends."

"Based on our historical financial data and current market conditions, predict our organization's financial performance for the next quarter."

"Examine our cash flow and working capital management to identify potential bottlenecks and areas for improvement."

By integrating AI technologies like GPT-4 into the financial analysis process, leaders can gain a deeper understanding of their organization's financial health, identify opportunities and challenges, and make more informed decisions to drive growth and success.

8.3 Risk Management and Compliance with AI

Risk management and compliance are essential aspects of financial management, as they help organizations identify, assess, and mitigate potential risks and adhere to relevant regulations. AI technologies like GPT-4 can play a significant role in enhancing risk management and compliance processes by providing timely and accurate insights. In this subchapter, we will explore the benefits of using AI to improve risk management and compliance in financial management.

Benefits of using AI for risk management and compliance:

1. **Enhanced risk identification:** AI can analyze vast amounts of data to identify potential risks and vulnerabilities in an organization's financial structure, allowing leaders to take proactive measures to mitigate these risks.

2. **Improved risk assessment:** AI can assess risks based on their likelihood and potential impact, helping leaders prioritize their risk mitigation efforts and allocate resources effectively.

3. **Streamlined compliance monitoring:** AI can monitor financial transactions and activities in real-time, ensuring that organizations comply with relevant regulations and avoid potential fines and penalties.

4. **Early warning systems:** AI can detect anomalies and red flags in financial data, alerting leaders to potential issues before they escalate and cause significant damage.

5. **Time and resource efficiency:** AI can automate various risk management and compliance tasks, reducing the workload for the finance team and allowing them to focus on other strategic tasks.

Example prompts for using AI in risk management and compliance:

"Analyze our financial data to identify potential risks and vulnerabilities in our organization's financial structure."

"Assess the likelihood and potential impact of identified risks and recommend appropriate mitigation strategies."

"Monitor our financial transactions and activities to ensure compliance with relevant regulations and identify potential issues."

"Detect anomalies and red flags in our financial data and alert us to potential issues before they escalate."

"Review our organization's internal controls and recommend improvements to enhance our risk management and compliance processes."

By leveraging AI technologies like GPT-4, leaders can significantly improve their organization's risk management and compliance processes, ensuring that they remain financially stable and adhere to relevant regulations.

8.4 Budgeting and Forecasting with AI

Budgeting and forecasting are crucial components of financial management, as they help organizations plan and allocate resources effectively. AI technologies like GPT-4 can significantly enhance budgeting and forecasting processes by providing accurate and data-driven insights that enable leaders to make informed decisions. In this subchapter, we will explore the benefits of using AI to improve budgeting and forecasting in financial management.

Benefits of using AI for budgeting and forecasting:

1. **Improved accuracy:** AI can analyze vast amounts of historical and real-time data to provide accurate and data-driven forecasts, reducing the likelihood of errors and increasing the reliability of financial predictions.

2. **Enhanced scenario analysis:** AI can simulate various scenarios and analyze their potential impact on the organization's financial performance, helping leaders make informed decisions and plan for contingencies.

3. **Time and resource efficiency:** AI can automate various budgeting and forecasting tasks, reducing the workload for the finance team and allowing them to focus on other strategic tasks.

4. **Real-time insights:** AI can continuously update budgeting and forecasting models with new data, providing leaders with real-time insights that enable them to respond quickly to changing market conditions and business needs.

5. **Data-driven decision-making:** AI can provide leaders with

actionable insights and recommendations, helping them make data-driven decisions and allocate resources effectively.

Example prompts for using AI in budgeting and forecasting:

```
"Analyze our historical financial data and generate a
detailed budget for the upcoming fiscal year."
```

```
"Forecast our organization's revenue and expenses for the
next quarter, considering current market conditions and
industry trends."
```

```
"Simulate various budget scenarios and analyze their
potential impact on our organization's financial
performance."
```

```
"Identify potential cost-saving opportunities and recommend
strategies to optimize our budget allocation."
```

"Provide real-time updates on our financial performance and
recommend adjustments to our budget and forecasts as needed."

By leveraging AI technologies like GPT-4, leaders can significantly
improve their organization's budgeting and forecasting processes,
ensuring that they plan and allocate resources effectively and respond
quickly to changing market conditions and business needs.

8.5 Risk Management and AI

Risk management is a critical aspect of financial management, as it
helps organizations identify, assess, and mitigate potential risks that
may impact their financial performance. AI technologies like GPT-4
can enhance risk management processes by providing data-driven
insights and predictive analytics that enable leaders to proactively
address potential risks and minimize their impact. In this subchapter,
we will discuss the benefits of using AI to improve risk management
in financial management.

Benefits of using AI for risk management:

1. **Early risk detection:** AI can analyze vast amounts of data to
   identify patterns and trends that may indicate potential risks,
   allowing organizations to address them proactively and minimize
   their impact.
2. **Improved risk assessment:** AI can assess the likelihood and
   potential impact of identified risks, enabling leaders to prioritize
   their risk mitigation efforts effectively.
3. **Enhanced risk mitigation strategies:** AI can provide data-
   driven insights and recommendations for addressing identified
   risks, helping organizations develop effective risk mitigation
   strategies.

4. **Continuous risk monitoring:** AI can continuously monitor various risk factors and provide real-time alerts and updates, allowing organizations to respond quickly to emerging risks and changing circumstances.

5. **Efficient risk reporting:** AI can automate the generation of risk reports and dashboards, providing leaders with a comprehensive view of their organization's risk profile and enabling them to make informed decisions.

Example prompts for using AI in risk management:

"Identify potential financial risks that our organization may face in the upcoming fiscal year, considering factors such as market volatility, regulatory changes, and industry trends."

"Assess the likelihood and potential impact of the identified risks and prioritize them based on their significance."

"Develop data-driven risk mitigation strategies for the identified risks and recommend steps to minimize their impact on our organization's financial performance."

"Monitor the identified risks continuously and provide
real-time alerts and updates on any significant changes or
emerging risks."

"Generate a comprehensive risk report that includes an
overview of our organization's risk profile, the status of
ongoing risk mitigation efforts, and recommendations for
future risk management initiatives."

By incorporating AI technologies like GPT-4 into their risk management processes, leaders can proactively address potential risks and minimize their impact on their organization's financial performance, ensuring long-term financial stability and success.

8.6 Budgeting and Forecasting with AI

Budgeting and forecasting are essential components of financial management, as they enable organizations to plan their financial resources effectively and anticipate future financial performance. AI technologies like GPT-4 can enhance budgeting and forecasting processes by providing data-driven insights, predictive analytics, and automation capabilities that streamline decision-making and improve the accuracy of financial projections. In this subchapter, we will discuss the benefits of using AI to improve budgeting and forecasting in financial management.

Benefits of using AI for budgeting and forecasting:

1. **Improved accuracy:** AI can analyze historical financial data, market trends, and industry-specific factors to generate more accurate financial projections, reducing the likelihood of budget

overruns and revenue shortfalls.

2. **Enhanced scenario analysis:** AI can model various financial scenarios and evaluate their potential impact on an organization's budget and financial performance, enabling leaders to make more informed decisions about resource allocation and strategic planning.

3. **Streamlined budgeting process:** AI can automate the collection and analysis of financial data, reducing the time and effort required to develop budgets and improving the efficiency of the budgeting process.

4. **Real-time financial insights:** AI can provide real-time updates on an organization's financial performance and budget variances, allowing leaders to quickly identify and address potential issues before they escalate.

5. **Adaptive forecasting:** AI can continuously update financial forecasts based on changing conditions and new information, ensuring that organizations remain agile and responsive to evolving market dynamics.

Example prompts for using AI in budgeting and forecasting:

```
"Analyze our historical financial data, market trends, and
industry-specific factors to generate an accurate financial
forecast for the upcoming fiscal year."
```

"Evaluate the potential impact of various financial
scenarios on our organization's budget and financial
performance, and recommend the most suitable resource
allocation strategy."

"Automate the collection and analysis of financial data
required for developing our annual budget, and generate a
comprehensive budget proposal for review and approval."

"Provide real-time updates on our organization's financial
performance and budget variances, and recommend corrective
actions to address any identified issues."

"Continuously update our financial forecasts based on
changing conditions and new information, ensuring that our
organization remains agile and responsive to evolving market
dynamics."

By leveraging AI technologies like GPT-4 in their budgeting and forecasting processes, leaders can improve the accuracy of their financial projections, streamline decision-making, and ensure the effective allocation of resources to support their organization's strategic objectives.

8.7 Risk Management and AI

Effective risk management is a critical aspect of financial management, as it enables organizations to identify, assess, and mitigate
potential threats to their financial stability and business objectives.
AI technologies like GPT-4 can play a crucial role in enhancing risk
management processes by providing advanced analytics, predictive
modeling, and real-time monitoring capabilities that support more
informed decision-making and proactive risk mitigation. In this
subchapter, we will discuss the benefits of using AI to improve risk
management in financial management.

Benefits of using AI for risk management:

1. **Advanced risk identification:** AI can analyze vast amounts
   of data from multiple sources to identify potential risks and
   vulnerabilities that may impact an organization's financial performance, including market trends, regulatory changes, and
   emerging industry threats.

2. **Enhanced risk assessment:** AI can evaluate the likelihood and
   potential impact of identified risks, enabling organizations to
   prioritize their risk mitigation efforts and allocate resources more
   effectively.

3. **Predictive risk modeling:** AI can develop predictive models
   that forecast the potential consequences of various risk scenarios,
   allowing organizations to assess the potential impact of their risk
   mitigation strategies and make more informed decisions about
   their risk management approach.

4. **Real-time risk monitoring:** AI can continuously monitor an
   organization's financial performance and risk exposure, providing real-time alerts and insights that enable leaders to take swift
   action to address emerging risks.

5. **Streamlined risk reporting:** AI can automate the generation
of risk reports and dashboards, simplifying the risk management
process and ensuring that leaders have access to up-to-date
information about their organization's risk profile.

Example prompts for using AI in risk management:

"Analyze our organization's financial data, market trends,
and regulatory environment to identify potential risks and
vulnerabilities that may impact our financial performance."

"Assess the likelihood and potential impact of identified
risks, and prioritize our risk mitigation efforts based on
their potential consequences."

"Develop predictive models that forecast the potential
consequences of various risk scenarios, and evaluate the
effectiveness of our risk mitigation strategies."

"Monitor our organization's financial performance and risk
exposure in real-time, and provide alerts and insights to
help us address emerging risks proactively."

```
"Automate the generation of risk reports and dashboards,
ensuring that our leadership team has access to up-to-date
information about our organization's risk profile."
```

By incorporating AI technologies like GPT-4 into their risk management processes, leaders can enhance their ability to identify, assess, and mitigate potential threats to their organization's financial stability and strategic objectives, ultimately fostering greater resilience and long-term success.

8.8 Prompt Templates for Financial Management Scenarios

In this subchapter, we will provide a collection of prompt templates that can be used to assist with various financial management tasks.

Financial Performance Analysis

```
"Analyze our organization's financial performance for the
last [time period] and identify key areas where improvements
can be made."
```

Use this prompt template to analyze your organization's financial performance and identify areas of improvement.

Expense Tracking and Analysis

```
"Track and analyze expenses for our organization over the
past [time period] and identify any areas where cost-saving
opportunities may exist."
```

This prompt template helps you track and analyze your organization's expenses, making it easier to identify cost-saving opportunities.

Revenue Forecasting

"Forecast our organization's revenues for the next [time period] based on historical data and industry trends."

Use this prompt template to forecast your organization's future revenues based on historical data and industry trends.

Cash Flow Analysis

"Analyze our organization's cash flow for the last [time period] and provide recommendations for maintaining optimal liquidity and financial stability."

This prompt template assists with analyzing your organization's cash flow to ensure optimal liquidity and financial stability.

Financial Risk Assessment

"Assess the financial risks facing our organization and provide recommendations for strategies to mitigate these risks."

Use this prompt template to assess the financial risks facing your organization and develop strategies to mitigate them.

Cost-Benefit Analysis

"Conduct a cost-benefit analysis for [project or initiative] and provide recommendations on whether to proceed with it or not."

This prompt template helps you conduct a cost-benefit analysis for a specific project or initiative.

Capital Investment Analysis

"Analyze the expected ROI for [capital investment] and provide recommendations on whether to proceed with the investment."

Use this prompt template to analyze potential capital investments and determine their expected return on investment (ROI).

Break-Even Analysis

"Calculate the break-even point for [product or service] based on its costs and revenues, and provide recommendations for pricing and production strategies."

This prompt template assists with determining the break-even point for a product or service, helping you make informed pricing and production decisions.

Financial Trend Analysis

"Identify and analyze the most significant financial trends affecting our industry and assess their potential impact on

```
our organization's performance."
```

Use this prompt template to analyze financial trends and their potential impact on your organization's performance.

Budget Variance Analysis

```
"Analyze the variances between our budgeted and actual
expenses for the last [time period] and identify the causes
of these variances."
```

This prompt template helps you analyze budget variances and determine their causes, enabling you to make necessary adjustments.

Financial Ratio Analysis

```
"Calculate and analyze the following financial ratios for
our organization: [list specific ratios] and provide
insights into our overall financial health."
```

Use this prompt template to calculate and analyze key financial ratios, providing insights into your organization's overall financial health.

Competitive Financial Analysis

```
"Analyze the financial performance of our top [number]
competitors in the [industry] and compare it to our own
performance, highlighting areas where we can improve."
```

This prompt template helps you analyze the financial performance of your competitors, allowing you to benchmark your organization's performance and identify areas for improvement.

Profit Margin Analysis

"Analyze our organization's profit margins by product, service, or division and identify opportunities to increase profitability."

Use this prompt template to analyze your organization's profit margins, identifying opportunities to increase profitability.

Working Capital Management

"Analyze our organization's working capital management and provide recommendations for optimizing the balance between liquidity and profitability."

This prompt template assists with optimizing your organization's working capital management, ensuring a healthy balance between liquidity and profitability.

Debt Management Analysis

"Analyze our organization's debt management strategies and provide recommendations for improving our debt profile."

Use this prompt template to analyze your organization's debt management strategies and identify opportunities to improve your debt profile.

Investment Portfolio Analysis

"Analyze our organization's investment portfolio and provide
recommendations for diversification and risk mitigation."

This prompt template helps you analyze your organization's investment portfolio, identifying opportunities for diversification and risk mitigation.

Pricing Strategy Analysis

"Analyze our organization's current pricing strategies and
provide recommendations for optimizing pricing to increase
revenue and profitability."

Use this prompt template to analyze your organization's pricing strategies, identifying opportunities to optimize pricing for increased revenue and profitability.

Financial Benchmarking

"Benchmark our organization's financial performance against
industry standards or top competitors and identify areas
where we can improve."

This prompt template assists with benchmarking your organization's financial performance against industry standards or competitors, helping you identify areas for improvement.

Mergers and Acquisitions Analysis

```
"Analyze the strategic fit and financial implications of a
potential merger or acquisition with [company name] and
provide recommendations on whether to proceed."
```

Use this prompt template to analyze potential mergers and acquisitions, assessing their strategic fit and financial implications.

Tax Planning Strategies

```
"Identify and analyze tax planning strategies that can help
our organization optimize tax liabilities and ensure
compliance."
```

This prompt template helps you explore tax planning strategies to optimize your organization's tax liabilities and ensure compliance.

By using these prompt templates, you can leverage AI for various financial management tasks, ultimately helping you make more informed decisions and drive better business outcomes.

9

Fostering Innovation and Managing Change through AI

I n today's rapidly evolving business landscape, innovation and change management are critical for organizational success. Artificial intelligence (AI) can play a pivotal role in promoting innovation and managing change effectively. This chapter will explore the ways AI can enhance leadership's ability to foster innovation and manage change within an organization. The subchapters will dive deeper into specific areas of focus, including:

1. **Identifying Emerging Trends and Technologies:** Discover how AI can help leaders identify and monitor emerging trends and technologies, enabling organizations to stay ahead of the curve and capitalize on new opportunities.

2. **Idea Generation and Evaluation:** Learn how AI can be utilized to generate innovative ideas, as well as evaluate and prioritize them based on factors such as feasibility, cost, and potential impact.

3. **Developing a Culture of Innovation:** Explore the ways AI can help leaders create a culture that encourages innovation

and supports experimentation, ultimately driving growth and competitiveness.

4. **Change Management and AI:** Understand how AI can aid in effective change management by providing insights, facilitating communication, and assisting in the implementation of change initiatives.

5. **AI in Organizational Restructuring:** Learn how AI can help organizations navigate restructuring, mergers, and acquisitions by providing insights and recommendations on the optimal structure and resource allocation.

6. **Monitoring and Adapting to Change:** Discover how AI can support leaders in monitoring the progress of change initiatives, identifying potential issues, and adapting strategies as needed to ensure success.

7. **AI and the Future of Work:** Examine the role of AI in shaping the future of work, including its impact on workforce planning, skills development, and employee engagement.

8. **Prompt Templates for Innovation and Change Management:** A variety of AI prompt templates designed to support leaders in fostering innovation and managing change within their organizations. These templates can be used as a starting point for generating insights, identifying areas for improvement, and developing targeted strategies for successful transformation.

Additional subchapters may be added to further explore the ways AI can enhance leadership's ability to foster innovation and manage change effectively. By leveraging AI, leaders can make more informed decisions, create a culture of innovation, and navigate change more successfully.

9.1 Identifying Emerging Trends and Technologies

In this subchapter, we will explore how AI can help leaders identify and monitor emerging trends and technologies. Staying ahead of the curve and capitalizing on new opportunities is essential for any organization's success. AI-driven tools and systems can provide invaluable insights and support informed decision-making in a rapidly changing environment.

Key Points:

1. The importance of monitoring emerging trends and technologies for organizations.
2. How AI-driven tools can identify and track trends, technologies, and market shifts.
3. Examples of AI-powered tools and platforms that facilitate trend identification and monitoring.
4. Ways to integrate AI-driven insights into organizational decision-making processes.

Example Prompts:

```
How can AI help leaders identify emerging trends and
technologies in their industry?
```

What are some examples of AI-driven tools or platforms that can assist in tracking trends and technologies?

How can organizations make better decisions using AI-driven insights into emerging trends and market shifts?

What challenges might leaders face when integrating AI-powered tools for trend identification into their decision-making processes?

How can organizations stay agile and adaptable in the face of rapid technological advancements and emerging trends?

By examining the use of AI in identifying emerging trends and technologies, leaders can better understand how to leverage these powerful tools to maintain a competitive edge in their industry. The insights and examples provided in this subchapter will help leaders effectively integrate AI-driven tools and platforms into their decision-making processes, ensuring they stay ahead of the curve and capitalize on new opportunities.

9.2 Idea Generation and Evaluation

In this subchapter, we will discuss the role of AI in generating innovative ideas and evaluating their potential impact on an organization. Leveraging AI-driven tools can help leaders develop a more comprehensive understanding of the feasibility, cost, and potential benefits of various ideas, allowing for more informed decision-making.

Key Points:

1. The importance of idea generation and evaluation in driving innovation.
2. How AI-driven tools can be utilized to generate innovative ideas and assess their potential impact.
3. Examples of AI-powered tools and platforms that facilitate idea generation and evaluation.
4. Strategies for integrating AI-driven insights into the decision-making process for innovation initiatives.

Example Prompts:

```
How can AI-driven tools assist leaders in generating
innovative ideas for their organization?
```

What are some examples of AI-powered platforms that can help evaluate the feasibility, cost, and potential impact of various ideas?

How can organizations effectively incorporate AI-driven insights into the decision-making process for innovation initiatives?

What challenges might leaders face when using AI-driven tools for idea generation and evaluation?

How can organizations foster a culture of innovation by leveraging AI-powered tools and platforms for idea generation and evaluation?

This subchapter will provide leaders with a comprehensive understanding of the role of AI in idea generation and evaluation. By exploring various AI-driven tools and platforms, leaders can learn how to effectively utilize these technologies to generate innovative ideas and assess their potential impact on their organization. Ultimately, this will enable leaders to make more informed decisions and drive growth and competitiveness within their organization.

9.3 Developing a Culture of Innovation

Creating a culture that encourages innovation and supports experimentation is crucial for organizational growth and competitiveness. In this subchapter, we will explore how AI can help leaders foster a culture of innovation within their organization, by providing insights, promoting collaboration, and streamlining processes.

Key Points:

1. The importance of cultivating a culture of innovation within an organization.
2. How AI can help leaders identify and remove barriers to innovation.
3. Ways in which AI-driven tools can facilitate collaboration and knowledge sharing among team members.
4. The role of AI in streamlining processes and promoting efficient experimentation.
5. Strategies for effectively leveraging AI to build and maintain a culture of innovation.

Example Prompts:

```
What are the key elements of a culture of innovation, and
why is it important for organizations to foster such a
culture?
```

How can AI-driven tools help leaders identify and remove barriers to innovation within their organization?

In what ways can AI facilitate collaboration and knowledge sharing among team members, promoting a culture of innovation?

How can AI streamline processes and promote efficient experimentation, driving innovation within an organization?

What strategies can leaders implement to effectively leverage AI in building and maintaining a culture of innovation?

By delving into the ways AI can be utilized to create a culture of innovation, this subchapter will provide leaders with the necessary knowledge and strategies to effectively leverage AI-driven tools and platforms. Through the promotion of collaboration, knowledge sharing, and efficient experimentation, AI can play a pivotal role in fostering an innovative culture that ultimately drives growth and competitiveness.

9.4 Change Management and AI

Change management is a crucial aspect of leadership, as organizations must continually adapt to shifting market conditions and internal developments. AI can play a significant role in facilitating effective change management, providing valuable insights, streamlining communication, and assisting in the implementation of change initiatives. This subchapter will delve into the various ways AI can aid leaders in managing change more effectively.

Key Points:

1. Understanding the challenges of change management and the importance of addressing these challenges to ensure organizational success.
2. The role of AI in providing data-driven insights to support decision-making during change management processes.
3. Leveraging AI-powered tools to facilitate communication and collaboration among stakeholders during change initiatives.
4. Using AI to assist in the implementation of change initiatives, including resource allocation, timeline management, and progress tracking.
5. How AI can help in identifying potential issues during the change process and suggesting corrective actions to address them.
6. Examples of successful change management initiatives that have benefited from the integration of AI technologies.

Example Prompts:

How can AI-powered analytics tools help leaders make data-driven decisions during change management processes?

In what ways can AI facilitate communication and collaboration among team members during a change initiative?

How can AI be used to track the progress of change initiatives and identify potential issues that may arise during implementation?

Provide an example of a successful change management initiative that leveraged AI technology to enhance its effectiveness.

Discuss the potential benefits of incorporating AI into change management strategies for organizations in various industries.

9.5 AI in Organizational Restructuring

Organizational restructuring, mergers, and acquisitions are often necessary for businesses to remain competitive and adapt to changing market conditions. AI can play a vital role in these processes by providing insights and recommendations on optimal organizational structure, resource allocation, and talent management. This subchapter will explore the various ways AI can support leaders in successfully navigating organizational restructuring and related changes.

Key Points:

1. The challenges and complexities involved in organizational restructuring, mergers, and acquisitions, and the importance of effective leadership in ensuring successful outcomes.
2. The role of AI in analyzing historical data, current market trends, and other relevant factors to provide actionable insights for restructuring decisions.
3. Leveraging AI-powered tools to evaluate and optimize organizational structures, including reporting lines, departmental divisions, and resource allocation.
4. Utilizing AI to support talent management during restructuring, including identifying high-potential employees, predicting retention risks, and recommending skill development initiatives.
5. The potential benefits of integrating AI into organizational restructuring efforts, including increased efficiency, reduced costs, and improved decision-making.
6. Case studies of successful organizational restructuring initiatives that have incorporated AI technologies to enhance outcomes.

Example Prompts:

How can AI help leaders make informed decisions about organizational structure and resource allocation during restructuring initiatives?

In what ways can AI-powered tools assist in identifying and retaining high-potential employees during mergers and acquisitions?

Discuss the potential benefits of incorporating AI into talent management strategies during organizational restructuring processes.

Provide an example of a successful organizational restructuring initiative that leveraged AI technology to improve efficiency and reduce costs.

How can AI be used to predict and address potential challenges and risks associated with organizational

```
restructuring, mergers, and acquisitions?
```

9.6 Monitoring and Adapting to Change

Innovation and change management are ongoing processes that require continuous monitoring and adaptation. AI can support leaders in tracking the progress of change initiatives, identifying potential issues, and adjusting strategies as needed to ensure success. This subchapter will discuss the various ways AI can be utilized to monitor and adapt to change, as well as the benefits of integrating AI into change management practices.

Key Points:

1. The importance of continuous monitoring and adaptation in successful change management and the role of AI in supporting these efforts.
2. The use of AI-powered analytics and tracking tools to monitor the progress of change initiatives, identifying potential issues and opportunities for improvement.
3. Leveraging AI to analyze employee feedback and sentiment data, allowing leaders to address concerns and better understand the impact of change on the workforce.
4. The role of AI in predicting potential risks and challenges associated with change initiatives, enabling proactive risk mitigation strategies.
5. The benefits of integrating AI into change management practices, including improved decision-making, increased agility, and enhanced organizational resilience.

Example Prompts:

Discuss the importance of continuous monitoring and adaptation in successful change management and the ways AI can support these efforts.

Describe how AI-powered analytics and tracking tools can help leaders monitor the progress of change initiatives and identify potential issues.

Explain the role of AI in analyzing employee feedback and sentiment data during change management processes, and how this information can be used to improve outcomes.

Provide an example of a change management initiative that successfully leveraged AI to predict potential risks and challenges, enabling proactive risk mitigation strategies.

How can integrating AI into change management practices contribute to improved decision-making, increased agility, and enhanced organizational resilience?

9.7 AI and the Future of Work

The future of work is rapidly evolving, and AI is expected to play a significant role in shaping the way organizations operate and employees engage with their tasks. This subchapter will explore the impact of AI on workforce planning, skills development, and employee engagement, and discuss how leaders can leverage AI to navigate the changing landscape of work.

Key Points:

1. The increasing integration of AI and automation in the workplace and its implications for workforce planning, including job displacement and the creation of new roles.
2. The importance of identifying the skills required for the future of work and how AI can assist leaders in understanding and addressing skills gaps.
3. The role of AI in facilitating personalized and adaptive learning, promoting continuous skills development and enhancing employee engagement.
4. The potential for AI to improve employee experience by automating repetitive tasks, enabling employees to focus on higher-value, more strategic work.
5. The ethical considerations surrounding the adoption of AI in the workplace, including concerns around privacy, fairness, and transparency.

Example Prompts:

Discuss the impact of AI on workforce planning, including potential job displacement and the creation of new roles. How can leaders prepare for these changes?

Explain the importance of identifying and addressing skills gaps in the context of the future of work, and describe how AI can assist leaders in this process.

Describe the role of AI in facilitating personalized and adaptive learning, and how this can contribute to continuous skills development and employee engagement.

Provide an example of how AI can improve employee experience by automating repetitive tasks, allowing employees to focus on higher-value work.

Discuss the ethical considerations surrounding the adoption of AI in the workplace and the responsibilities of leaders in addressing these concerns.

9.8 Prompt Templates for Innovation and Change Management

In this subchapter, we will provide a variety of AI prompt templates designed to support leaders in fostering innovation and managing change within their organizations. These templates can be used as a starting point for generating insights, identifying areas for improvement, and developing targeted strategies for successful transformation.

Identifying opportunities for innovation:

"Analyze our organization's current situation and identify potential opportunities for innovation."

Use this prompt template to help identify areas within your organization where innovation may be beneficial.

Assessing the impact of new ideas:

"Evaluate the impact and feasibility of the following innovative idea: [insert idea here]."

This prompt template helps evaluate the potential impact and feasibility of new ideas and initiatives.

Brainstorming innovative solutions:

```
"Brainstorm innovative solutions to address the following
challenge: [insert challenge here]."
```

Use this prompt template to generate a list of creative solutions to address specific challenges or opportunities within your organization.

Developing an innovation strategy:

```
"Develop a comprehensive innovation strategy for our
organization, including objectives, required resources, and
potential barriers."
```

This prompt template helps outline the key components of an innovation strategy, including objectives, resources, and potential barriers.

Assessing change readiness:

```
"Analyze our organization's readiness for change and
identify any areas that may require additional preparation."
```

Use this prompt template to determine the readiness of your organization for change and identify any areas that may require additional preparation.

Creating a change management plan:

```
"Create a detailed change management plan for our
organization, including goals, stakeholders, and required
steps."
```

This prompt template helps develop a detailed change management plan, outlining the goals, stakeholders, and steps necessary to achieve successful transformation.

Monitoring and evaluating change initiatives:

"Monitor and evaluate the progress of our change initiative, and suggest any necessary adjustments to our plans."

Use this prompt template to track the progress of change initiatives and adjust plans based on real-time feedback.

Encouraging a culture of innovation:

"Suggest strategies to encourage a culture of innovation within our organization."

This prompt template helps identify strategies to promote a culture of innovation within your organization.

Identifying barriers to innovation:

"Identify potential barriers or obstacles preventing innovation within our organization."

This prompt template helps identify any barriers or obstacles that may be preventing innovation within your organization.

Prioritizing innovative projects:

"Prioritize the following innovative projects based on their potential impact, cost, and feasibility: [list projects]."

Use this prompt template to help prioritize various innovative projects based on factors such as impact, cost, and feasibility.

Identifying and engaging stakeholders:

"Identify key stakeholders for our change initiative and suggest strategies for engaging them effectively."

This prompt template helps identify key stakeholders in change initiatives and strategies for engaging them effectively.

Evaluating the effectiveness of change communication:

"Evaluate the effectiveness of our organization's change communication efforts and suggest areas for improvement."

Use this prompt template to assess the effectiveness of your organization's change communication efforts and suggest improvements.

Analyzing the risks of innovation:

"Analyze potential risks associated with the following innovative project: [insert project here]."

This prompt template helps analyze potential risks associated with innovative projects and initiatives.

Aligning innovation with organizational goals:

"Ensure that our innovative project, [insert project name],
aligns with our organization's goals and objectives."

Use this prompt template to ensure that innovative projects are aligned with your organization's overarching goals and objectives.

Assessing the success of implemented innovations:

"Assess the success of the implemented innovation, [insert
innovation name], by measuring its impact on key performance
indicators."

This prompt template helps assess the success of implemented innovations by measuring their impact on key performance indicators.

Fostering cross-functional collaboration:

"Identify strategies for fostering cross-functional
collaboration within our organization to drive innovation."

Use this prompt template to identify strategies for promoting cross-functional collaboration to drive innovation within your organization.

Building an innovation pipeline:

"Create a pipeline of innovative ideas and projects for our
organization that can be continuously evaluated and
developed."

This prompt template helps create a pipeline of innovative ideas and projects that can be continuously evaluated and developed.

Overcoming resistance to change:

"Identify potential sources of resistance to our change initiative and develop strategies to overcome them."

Use this prompt template to identify potential sources of resistance to change and develop strategies to overcome them.

Developing innovation metrics:

"Develop a set of innovation metrics to track progress and evaluate the effectiveness of our organization's innovation efforts."

This prompt template helps create measurable indicators of innovation success to track progress and evaluate the effectiveness of your organization's innovation efforts.

Creating a learning culture:

"Identify strategies for creating a learning culture within our organization to promote continuous improvement and adaptability."

Use this prompt template to identify strategies for creating a learning culture within your organization, promoting continuous improvement and adaptability.

These AI prompt templates can be customized to fit your specific organizational context, helping leaders leverage AI's capabilities to foster innovation and manage change effectively. By utilizing these prompts, leaders can better anticipate challenges, develop targeted strategies, and drive successful transformations that propel their organizations forward.

10

Ethical Leadership in the Age of AI

I n Chapter 10, we will explore the critical topic of ethical
leadership in the age of AI. As AI becomes increasingly integrated
into various aspects of organizational operations, leaders must
ensure that they uphold ethical standards and principles. This chapter
will discuss the importance of ethical leadership and provide guidance
on developing and implementing ethical AI practices. The subchapters
included in this chapter are:

1. **Understanding the Importance of Ethical Leadership in
   the Age of AI:** This subchapter will discuss the significance of
   ethical leadership as AI becomes more prevalent in organizations,
   touching on the potential implications of AI on privacy, fairness,
   and transparency.
2. **Establishing Ethical AI Guidelines and Frameworks:** In this
   section, we will explore how organizations can create ethical AI
   guidelines and frameworks to ensure that AI is used responsibly
   and ethically.
3. **Training and Education in Ethical AI:** This subchapter will
   delve into the importance of training and education for leaders

and employees in ethical AI practices, equipping them with the knowledge and skills needed to make responsible decisions regarding AI deployment.

4. **Ethical AI Governance Frameworks:** In this section, we will discuss the role of governance frameworks in promoting ethical AI practices, providing guidance on creating effective governance structures to oversee AI usage within organizations.

5. **Prompt Templates for Ethical Decision-making:** In this section, we will provide prompt templates designed to facilitate ethical decision-making in AI-related scenarios, empowering leaders to tackle complex ethical dilemmas and make responsible choices.

Throughout this chapter, our aim is to offer a comprehensive understanding of ethical leadership in the context of AI, providing leaders with the tools and insights needed to navigate the complex ethical landscape and ensure responsible AI deployment within their organizations.

10.1 Understanding the Importance of Ethical Leadership in the Age of AI

In this subchapter, we will explore the significance of ethical leadership in the context of AI adoption and the potential consequences of ignoring ethical considerations. As AI continues to transform industries and decision-making processes, ethical leadership plays a critical role in ensuring responsible AI use that benefits both organizations and society.

The increasing role of AI in decision-making: Discuss the growing reliance on AI systems for various aspects of business operations, from strategic planning to human resources, and the importance of ethical leadership in overseeing these technologies.

Example prompt:

```
"How has the role of AI in decision-making evolved, and what
responsibilities do leaders have in ensuring ethical AI use
in their organizations?"
```

The consequences of unethical AI use: Examine the potential negative impacts of AI systems that lack ethical considerations, such as biased decision-making, loss of public trust, and regulatory penalties.

Example prompt:

"What are the potential consequences of unethical AI use for
organizations and society at large?"

Balancing innovation and ethics: Explore the delicate balance that leaders need to strike between fostering innovation and ensuring ethical AI use, taking into account the potential risks and rewards.

Example prompt:

"How can leaders balance the need for innovation with the
responsibility to ensure ethical AI use in their
organizations?"

Developing an ethical AI strategy: Discuss the role of leaders in creating and implementing an ethical AI strategy within their organizations, including the establishment of AI governance structures and policies.

Example prompt:

"What are the key components of an ethical AI strategy, and
how can leaders successfully implement such a strategy in
their organizations?"

By exploring these topics, this subchapter aims to underscore the importance of ethical leadership in the age of AI and highlight the potential consequences of neglecting ethical considerations in AI adoption.

10.2 Establishing Ethical AI Guidelines and Frameworks

In this subchapter, we will delve into the process of creating ethical AI guidelines and frameworks that can guide organizations in developing and deploying AI systems responsibly. Leaders must not only be aware of ethical considerations but also take active steps to ensure their organizations adhere to established guidelines that promote transparency, fairness, and accountability in AI applications.

Reviewing existing ethical AI frameworks: Examine some of the existing ethical AI frameworks and guidelines put forth by various organizations and institutions, such as the European Union's AI Ethics Guidelines and the IEEE's Ethically Aligned Design.

Example prompt:

"What are some notable examples of ethical AI frameworks and guidelines, and what can we learn from them?"

Identifying core ethical principles: Discuss the core ethical principles that should guide the development and deployment of AI systems, such as fairness, transparency, accountability, and privacy.

Example prompt:

"What are the key ethical principles that should be considered when developing and deploying AI systems, and why are they important?"

Customizing guidelines for specific industries and use cases:
Explore the process of tailoring ethical AI guidelines to meet the
unique needs and challenges of specific industries and use cases, while
maintaining alignment with overarching ethical principles.

Example prompt:

"How can organizations customize ethical AI guidelines to
address the specific needs and challenges of their industry
or use case?"

Integrating ethical AI guidelines into organizational culture:
Discuss strategies for integrating ethical AI guidelines into an organization's culture and ensuring that these principles are upheld at every
level, from executive leadership to individual employees.

Example prompt:

"What steps can leaders take to ensure that ethical AI
guidelines are integrated into their organization's culture
and adhered to by all employees?"

This subchapter will provide insights into the process of establishing
ethical AI guidelines and frameworks, emphasizing the importance of
aligning AI development and deployment with core ethical principles
that promote responsible AI use.

10.3 Training and Education in Ethical AI

This subchapter will discuss the importance of training and education in ethical AI for both leaders and employees. As AI systems become more prevalent in various aspects of business, it is crucial that organizations invest in training and education programs to ensure that everyone understands the ethical implications and best practices associated with AI.

Developing ethical AI training programs: Discuss how organizations can design and implement comprehensive training programs that cover ethical AI principles, guidelines, and best practices.

Example prompt:

"What are the key components of an effective ethical AI training program, and how can organizations implement these programs to ensure understanding among employees?"

Encouraging a culture of continuous learning: Explore strategies for promoting a culture of continuous learning within organizations, emphasizing the importance of staying up to date with the latest developments in ethical AI.

Example prompt:

"How can organizations create a culture of continuous learning that emphasizes the importance of staying current with ethical AI developments and best practices?"

Addressing ethical dilemmas and decision-making: Discuss how training and education programs can help employees develop the skills needed to navigate ethical dilemmas and make informed decisions when faced with complex AI-related issues.

Example prompt:

"How can training and education in ethical AI help employees build the necessary skills to navigate ethical dilemmas and make responsible decisions in AI-related situations?"

Collaborating with external experts and organizations: Explore the benefits of collaborating with external experts and organizations in the field of ethical AI to enhance in-house training programs and stay abreast of the latest developments.

Example prompt:

"What are the advantages of collaborating with external experts and organizations in ethical AI to enhance an organization's training and education programs?"

This subchapter will provide insights into the importance of training and education in ethical AI, highlighting the need for comprehensive programs that ensure both leaders and employees are equipped to make responsible decisions and address ethical dilemmas related to AI systems.

10.4 Ethical AI Governance Frameworks

This subchapter will explore the importance of establishing ethical AI governance frameworks within organizations to ensure that AI systems are used responsibly and ethically. It will provide guidelines and best practices for developing and implementing these frameworks, as well as discuss the role of leadership in fostering a culture of ethical AI.

Components of an ethical AI governance framework: Discuss the key elements that should be included in an ethical AI governance framework, such as policies, guidelines, and oversight mechanisms.

Example prompt:

```
"What are the essential components of an ethical AI
governance framework, and how can organizations integrate
these elements to ensure responsible AI usage?"
```

Developing and implementing AI policies and guidelines: Explore the process of creating and implementing AI policies and guidelines that adhere to ethical principles and industry best practices.

Example prompt:

```
"How can organizations develop and implement AI policies and
guidelines that align with ethical principles and industry
best practices?"
```

Establishing oversight and monitoring mechanisms: Discuss
the importance of creating oversight and monitoring mechanisms
to ensure that AI systems are used ethically and responsibly.

Example prompt:

"What types of oversight and monitoring mechanisms should
organizations put in place to ensure ethical and responsible
AI usage?"

The role of leadership in fostering a culture of ethical AI: Examine
the responsibilities of organizational leaders in promoting a culture
of ethical AI and ensuring adherence to governance frameworks.

Example prompt:

"What is the role of leadership in fostering a culture of
ethical AI and ensuring compliance with AI governance
frameworks?"

By examining the various aspects of ethical AI governance frameworks,
this subchapter will provide guidance for organizations seeking to
develop and implement policies, guidelines, and oversight mechanisms
to ensure the responsible and ethical use of AI systems.

10.5 Prompt Templates for Ethical Decision-making

In this subchapter, we will provide a set of prompt templates to help leaders navigate ethical decision-making in the context of AI applications. These templates will cover various ethical dilemmas and scenarios that may arise while using AI systems and provide guidance to make informed and ethical choices.

Identifying potential ethical issues in AI projects

"What are the potential ethical issues in the following AI project: [project description]?"

Assessing fairness and bias in AI systems

"How can we assess and mitigate potential biases in the AI system we are developing for [specific use case]?"

Ensuring transparency and explainability in AI systems

"What steps can we take to ensure our AI system for [specific use case] is transparent and explainable to stakeholders?"

Evaluating privacy and data protection concerns

"What are the privacy and data protection implications of using AI in [specific use case], and how can we address them?"

Weighing the trade-offs between AI benefits and potential harms

"What are the potential benefits and harms of implementing
AI in [specific use case], and how can we weigh these
trade-offs to make an ethical decision?"

Aligning AI system development with organizational values

"How can we ensure that our AI system aligns with our
organization's values and ethical principles in [specific
use case]?"

Implementing responsible AI usage policies

"What policies should we put in place to ensure responsible
AI usage in our organization?"

Responding to unintended consequences of AI

"How should our organization respond to the unintended
consequences of our AI system in [specific use case], and
what steps can we take to prevent future issues?"

Engaging with stakeholders on ethical AI concerns

"How can we engage with stakeholders to address their
ethical concerns related to our AI system in [specific use
case]?"

Developing an AI ethics training program

"What are the key components of an AI ethics training program for our organization, and how can we implement it effectively?"

Monitoring AI systems for ethical compliance

"What monitoring and evaluation processes should we establish to ensure our AI system remains ethically compliant in [specific use case]?"

Engaging with external experts on AI ethics

"How can we collaborate with external experts to strengthen our organization's understanding and implementation of AI ethics?"

Considering the societal impact of AI applications

"What are the broader societal implications of our AI system in [specific use case], and how can we address them responsibly?"

Ensuring accessibility and inclusiveness in AI systems

"How can we make our AI system for [specific use case] accessible and inclusive to diverse user groups?"

Establishing a code of ethics for AI development

"What should be included in our organization's code of
ethics for AI development and deployment?"

Assessing the environmental impact of AI systems

"What are the environmental implications of our AI system in
[specific use case], and how can we minimize its ecological
footprint?"

Addressing ethical concerns in AI partnerships

"How can we ensure ethical alignment with our AI technology
partners and suppliers?"

Developing an AI ethics committee or advisory board

"What are the roles and responsibilities of an AI ethics
committee or advisory board in our organization, and how
should we establish it?"

Creating a culture of ethical AI development

"What steps can we take to foster a culture of ethical AI
development within our organization?"

Evaluating the long-term ethical implications of AI systems

"How can we assess and plan for the long-term ethical
implications of our AI system in [specific use case]?"

These templates serve as a starting point for leaders to address the ethical considerations of AI applications in their organizations. They can be modified and adapted to fit the specific needs and contexts of different organizations and scenarios.

11

Performance Evaluation with AI Assistance

P erformance evaluation is a critical aspect of leadership and plays a significant role in the growth and development of both employees and organizations. In the age of AI, performance evaluation has evolved, and AI-assisted systems have emerged as valuable tools for leaders to assess and improve employee performance. This chapter will delve into the various aspects of performance evaluation with AI assistance, examining the importance of this approach and discussing how it can be implemented effectively within an organization.

Subchapters will cover topics such as:

1. **Understanding the Importance of Performance Evaluation in the Age of AI:** Explore the role of AI in enhancing the performance evaluation process and the benefits it offers for leaders and employees alike.

2. **Key Components of AI-Assisted Performance Evaluation Systems:** Learn about the essential elements of AI-assisted performance evaluation systems, including data sources, algorithms,

and feedback mechanisms.

3. **Best Practices for Implementing AI-Assisted Performance Evaluation Systems:** Examine the best practices for implementing these systems, including integrating them with existing performance management processes and ensuring transparency and fairness.

4. **Addressing Potential Challenges and Biases in AI-Assisted Performance Evaluation:** Discuss the potential issues and biases that may arise in AI-assisted performance evaluation systems and how to mitigate them.

5. **Continuous Improvement and Adaptation in AI-Assisted Performance Evaluation Systems:** Understand how to continuously improve and adapt AI-assisted performance evaluation systems, ensuring they remain effective and relevant over time.

6. **Training and Development Opportunities through AI-Assisted Performance Evaluations:** Discover how AI-assisted performance evaluations can be used to identify training and development opportunities for employees, facilitating their growth and improvement.

7. **Prompt Templates for Performance Evaluation:** Learn about various prompt templates that can be used for AI-assisted performance evaluations, allowing for more efficient and effective assessments.

By incorporating AI into performance evaluations, leaders can make better-informed decisions, improve employee performance, and drive overall organizational success. This chapter will provide a comprehensive understanding of AI-assisted performance evaluation systems and offer guidance on how to implement them effectively in a leadership context.

11.1 Understanding the Importance of Performance Evaluation in the Age of AI

The importance of performance evaluation in the age of AI cannot be overstated. With remote and hybrid work arrangements becoming increasingly prevalent, employee expectations are evolving. It is crucial for organizations to adapt their performance evaluation processes to meet these changing needs. By harnessing the power of AI, companies can provide more accurate and objective assessments of employee performance.

One of the key benefits of AI-driven performance evaluations is the ability to collect and analyze vast amounts of data. This data-driven approach allows for more objective assessments, helping to reduce human biases and errors that may otherwise influence evaluations. As a result, organizations can make more informed decisions about employee development, promotions, and other talent management initiatives.

Example prompts:

"How can AI be used to improve the objectivity of performance evaluations?"

"What are the potential pitfalls of using AI in performance evaluation processes?"

"How can organizations ensure fairness and equity in AI-driven performance evaluations?"

"What are the benefits of using AI to provide continuous feedback and development for employees?"

However, it is essential to recognize that AI can also perpetuate biases if not carefully designed and managed. Ensuring fairness in AI-driven performance evaluation systems is crucial, as it helps create a more inclusive and equitable work environment. By addressing potential biases in AI systems, organizations can promote diversity and foster a more inclusive culture.

AI-driven performance evaluations can also facilitate continuous feedback and development. By providing real-time insights into employee performance, AI-powered systems can help employees identify areas of improvement and receive ongoing support from their managers. This real-time feedback loop can ultimately lead to increased employee engagement and satisfaction.

Remember to consider the ethical implications of using AI in performance evaluation processes, as well as the potential impact on employee morale and trust. By carefully considering these factors, organizations can harness the power of AI to enhance their performance evaluation processes and create a more equitable and inclusive work environment.

11.2 Key Components of AI-Assisted Performance Evaluation Systems

AI-assisted performance evaluation systems can provide organizations with a more efficient and effective means of assessing employee performance. By integrating key components into their performance evaluation processes, organizations can ensure that their AI-driven systems are both fair and reliable.

Data Collection and Analysis:

A robust AI-driven performance evaluation system relies on the collection and analysis of various data points related to employee performance. This may include quantitative metrics, such as sales figures or project completion rates, as well as qualitative data, such as feedback from peers and supervisors. The AI system should be able to collect and process this data in a way that provides a comprehensive picture of an employee's performance.

Example prompts:

```
"What types of data should be collected for an AI-driven
performance evaluation system?"
```

```
"How can organizations ensure the data used in AI-driven
performance evaluations is accurate and relevant?"
```

Objective Metrics and Criteria:

To minimize bias and ensure fairness, AI-assisted performance evaluation systems should use objective metrics and criteria. This means establishing clear performance indicators and benchmarks that can be consistently applied across the organization. By using objective metrics, organizations can reduce the impact of human biases in the evaluation process.

Example prompts:

"What are some examples of objective performance metrics that can be used in AI-driven performance evaluations?"

"How can organizations establish and maintain consistent evaluation criteria across different teams and departments?"

Feedback and Development Opportunities:

AI-assisted performance evaluation systems should incorporate real-time feedback and development opportunities. This can help employees identify areas for improvement and receive ongoing support from their managers. By providing a continuous feedback loop, organizations can promote employee engagement and satisfaction.

Example prompts:

"How can AI-driven performance evaluations facilitate continuous feedback and development?"

●

"What are some best practices for integrating real-time
feedback into AI-driven performance evaluation processes?"

Bias Detection and Mitigation:

To ensure fairness and equity, AI-assisted performance evaluation systems should be designed with bias detection and mitigation in mind. This involves regularly auditing the AI system to identify potential biases and taking steps to address them. By actively monitoring and addressing biases in AI-driven performance evaluations, organizations can promote diversity and foster a more inclusive work environment.

Example prompts:

"What are some common biases that can emerge in AI-driven
performance evaluations, and how can they be mitigated?"

"What role do data scientists and HR professionals play in
detecting and addressing biases in AI-assisted performance
evaluation systems?"

Employee Privacy and Trust:

Finally, it is essential to consider the impact of AI-driven performance evaluations on employee privacy and trust. Organizations should be transparent about how data is collected, analyzed, and used in the evaluation process. By maintaining open communication and addressing any employee concerns, organizations can build trust and ensure that their AI-driven performance evaluation systems are seen as fair and reliable.

Example prompts:

"How can organizations maintain employee privacy while using AI-driven performance evaluations?"

"What steps can be taken to build trust and transparency in the AI-assisted performance evaluation process?"

By incorporating these key components into their AI-assisted performance evaluation systems, organizations can improve the accuracy, fairness, and effectiveness of their performance management processes. This, in turn, can lead to a more engaged and productive workforce.

11.3 Best Practices for Implementing AI-Assisted Performance Evaluation Systems

When implementing AI-assisted performance evaluation systems, organizations should follow best practices to ensure the successful integration of AI technologies and the fair evaluation of employee performance. These best practices can help organizations optimize their performance management processes while minimizing potential pitfalls associated with AI-driven systems.

Collaborate with Key Stakeholders:

Collaborating with key stakeholders such as HR professionals, managers, and employees is essential for the successful implementation of an AI-assisted performance evaluation system. By involving these stakeholders in the decision-making process, organizations can ensure that the system is designed to meet the needs and expectations of all parties involved.

Example prompts:

```
"How can organizations involve key stakeholders in the
implementation of AI-driven performance evaluation systems?"
```

```
"What are the potential benefits of involving HR
professionals, managers, and employees in the development of
AI-driven performance evaluation processes?"
```

Customize the System to Meet Organizational Needs:
Each organization has unique performance management requirements. Therefore, it is crucial to customize AI-driven performance evaluation systems to align with the organization's specific goals, culture, and values. This may involve tailoring the system's data inputs, evaluation criteria, and feedback mechanisms to suit the organization's needs.

Example prompts:

"How can organizations customize AI-assisted performance evaluation systems to meet their specific needs and goals?"

"What factors should be considered when tailoring an AI-driven performance evaluation system to fit an organization's culture and values?"

Provide Training and Support:
Employees and managers should receive training and support to help them effectively use and navigate AI-driven performance evaluation systems. This may include training on system functionality, as well as guidance on interpreting and acting upon the feedback provided by the system.

Example prompts:

"What types of training and support should be provided to
employees and managers when implementing an AI-assisted
performance evaluation system?"

"How can organizations ensure that employees and managers
feel confident using AI-driven performance evaluation tools?"

Continuously Monitor and Update the System:

AI-assisted performance evaluation systems should be continuously monitored and updated to ensure their ongoing effectiveness and accuracy. This may involve auditing the system for potential biases, reviewing the data inputs and evaluation criteria, and making adjustments as needed to maintain alignment with organizational goals and values.

Example prompts:

"How can organizations monitor and update AI-driven
performance evaluation systems to ensure their continued
effectiveness?"

"What are the potential risks associated with not regularly
updating AI-assisted performance evaluation systems?"

Evaluate the System's Impact:

Finally, organizations should regularly evaluate the impact of their

AI-driven performance evaluation systems on employee performance, engagement, and satisfaction. This can help organizations identify areas for improvement and determine whether the system is delivering the desired outcomes.

Example prompts:

```
"What metrics can be used to evaluate the impact of an
AI-assisted performance evaluation system on employee
performance and engagement?"
```

```
"How can organizations use data and feedback to refine and
improve their AI-driven performance evaluation processes?"
```

By following these best practices, organizations can successfully implement AI-assisted performance evaluation systems that are both effective and fair. In turn, this can lead to more accurate performance assessments, improved employee engagement, and better overall organizational performance.

11.4 Addressing Potential Challenges and Biases in AI-Assisted Performance Evaluation

While AI-assisted performance evaluation systems offer many advantages, they can also present potential challenges and biases that organizations must address to ensure fair and accurate evaluations. By understanding these challenges and implementing strategies to overcome them, organizations can maximize the benefits of AI-driven performance evaluation while minimizing potential drawbacks.

Data Quality and Representativeness:

The accuracy and fairness of AI-assisted performance evaluation systems rely heavily on the quality and representativeness of the data used to train and inform the system. Inaccurate, incomplete, or biased data can lead to unfair and biased evaluations.

Example prompts:

```
"How can organizations ensure that the data used to train
and inform AI-driven performance evaluation systems is
accurate, complete, and representative?"
```

```
"What steps can be taken to address potential biases in the
data used for AI-assisted performance evaluation?"
```

Algorithmic Bias:

Algorithmic biases may emerge from biased data or flawed algorithms, which can result in unfair evaluations for certain employee groups. Organizations must be vigilant in identifying and addressing such biases in their AI-driven performance evaluation systems.

Example prompts:

"How can organizations identify and address algorithmic biases in their AI-assisted performance evaluation systems?"

"What strategies can be employed to minimize the risk of algorithmic bias in AI-driven performance evaluation?"

Transparency and Explainability:
AI-assisted performance evaluation systems should be transparent and explainable, allowing employees and managers to understand how performance assessments are generated. This is crucial for ensuring fairness and fostering trust in the system.

Example prompts:

"Why is transparency and explainability important in AI-driven performance evaluation systems?"

"How can organizations ensure that their AI-assisted performance evaluation processes are transparent and easily understood by employees and managers?"

Employee Privacy and Data Security:

Organizations must balance the use of AI-driven performance evaluation systems with the need to protect employee privacy and secure sensitive data. This may involve establishing clear data usage policies and implementing robust data security measures.

Example prompts:

"What steps can organizations take to protect employee privacy and secure sensitive data when using AI-assisted performance evaluation systems?"

"How can organizations balance the benefits of AI-driven performance evaluation with the need for employee privacy and data security?"

Legal and Ethical Considerations:

AI-assisted performance evaluation systems must comply with relevant legal and ethical guidelines, such as employment laws and data protection regulations. Organizations should consult with legal and HR experts to ensure compliance and minimize potential legal risks.

Example prompts:

"What legal and ethical considerations should organizations be aware of when implementing AI-driven performance evaluation systems?"

"How can organizations ensure that their AI-assisted performance evaluation processes comply with relevant laws and regulations?"

By addressing these potential challenges and biases, organizations can ensure that their AI-assisted performance evaluation systems are fair, accurate, and effective, leading to improved employee performance, engagement, and satisfaction.

11.5 Continuous Improvement and Adaptation in AI-Assisted Performance Evaluation Systems

As with any technology, AI-assisted performance evaluation systems require continuous improvement and adaptation to ensure their effectiveness and relevance over time. Organizations must invest time and resources into refining and updating their AI-driven performance evaluation processes to address evolving business needs, employee expectations, and technological advancements.

Regularly Assessing and Updating Evaluation Criteria:
Organizations should regularly assess and update the evaluation criteria used by their AI-driven performance evaluation systems to ensure that they remain relevant and aligned with business objectives.

Example prompts:

"How can organizations ensure that the evaluation criteria
used in AI-assisted performance evaluation systems remain
relevant and aligned with business objectives?"

"What processes can be implemented to regularly assess and
update evaluation criteria in AI-driven performance
evaluation systems?"

Monitoring and Addressing Emerging Biases:

As new data is incorporated into AI-assisted performance evaluation systems, new biases may emerge. Organizations must continuously monitor and address these biases to maintain fairness and accuracy in the evaluation process.

Example prompts:

"How can organizations monitor and address emerging biases
in AI-assisted performance evaluation systems?"

"What strategies can be employed to ensure that AI-driven
performance evaluation systems remain unbiased and fair over

time?"

Adapting to Changes in Employee Roles and Responsibilities:

As employee roles and responsibilities evolve, AI-driven performance evaluation systems should be updated to accurately assess and measure employee performance in their current roles.

Example prompts:

"How can organizations adapt AI-assisted performance
evaluation systems to address changes in employee roles and
responsibilities?

"What steps can be taken to ensure that AI-driven
performance evaluation systems remain relevant as employee
roles evolve over time?"

Incorporating Employee Feedback:

Organizations should actively seek and incorporate employee feedback into their AI-assisted performance evaluation systems to ensure that they remain fair, transparent, and accurate.

Example prompts:

"Why is employee feedback important in the continuous
improvement of AI-driven performance evaluation systems?"

"How can organizations effectively incorporate employee
feedback into their AI-assisted performance evaluation
processes?"

Staying Informed of Technological Advancements:

As AI technology continues to advance, organizations must stay
informed of the latest developments and incorporate them into
their performance evaluation processes to maximize the benefits and
effectiveness of AI-driven systems.

Example prompts:

"How can organizations stay informed of the latest
advancements in AI technology relevant to performance
evaluation?"

"What strategies can be employed to ensure that AI-assisted
performance evaluation systems benefit from ongoing
technological advancements?"

By continuously improving and adapting AI-assisted performance
evaluation systems, organizations can ensure that they remain effective, relevant, and fair, ultimately leading to better employee
performance, engagement, and satisfaction.

11.6 Training and Development Opportunities through AI-Assisted Performance Evaluations

AI-assisted performance evaluations not only help organizations assess employee performance but can also provide valuable insights into training and development opportunities. By analyzing employee strengths and weaknesses, AI-driven systems can identify areas where employees can benefit from additional training, skill development, or mentorship.

Identifying Skill Gaps:

AI-driven performance evaluation systems can help identify skill gaps and areas for improvement in employees, enabling organizations to tailor training and development programs to address these needs.

Example prompts:

```
"How can AI-assisted performance evaluations help
organizations identify skill gaps in their workforce?"
```

```
"What strategies can organizations use to address skill gaps
identified through AI-driven performance evaluations?"
```

Personalized Learning and Development Plans:

Leveraging AI-driven insights, organizations can create personalized learning and development plans for employees, focusing on their specific needs and career goals.

213

Example prompts:

"How can AI-assisted performance evaluations contribute to the development of personalized learning plans for employees?"

"What are the benefits of creating personalized learning and development plans based on AI-driven performance evaluation insights?"

Identifying High-Potential Employees:

AI-assisted performance evaluations can help organizations identify high-potential employees, who may benefit from targeted development programs and accelerated career progression opportunities.

Example prompts:

"How can AI-driven performance evaluations help organizations identify high-potential employees?"

"What strategies can be employed to develop and retain high-potential employees identified through AI-assisted performance evaluations?"

Continuous Feedback and Development:
AI-driven performance evaluation systems can provide continuous, real-time feedback to employees, enabling them to identify areas for improvement and track their progress over time.

Example prompts:

"How can AI-assisted performance evaluations support continuous feedback and development for employees?"

"What are the benefits of incorporating real-time feedback into AI-driven performance evaluation processes?"

Mentoring and Coaching Opportunities:
By analyzing employee performance data, AI-assisted evaluation systems can help organizations identify employees who may benefit from mentoring or coaching relationships, fostering collaboration and knowledge sharing within the organization.

Example prompts:

"How can AI-driven performance evaluations support the establishment of mentoring and coaching relationships within an organization?"

"What are the benefits of leveraging AI-assisted performance
evaluations to identify and facilitate mentoring
opportunities?"

By utilizing AI-driven insights from performance evaluations, organizations can create targeted and effective training and development
programs, ultimately leading to a more skilled, engaged, and productive workforce.

11.7 Prompt Templates for Performance Evaluation

Identifying Strengths and Areas for Improvement:

"What are [Employee]'s top three strengths, and how can they
further leverage these to contribute to the team's success?"

"Which areas could [Employee] focus on for improvement, and
what steps should be taken to address these areas?"

Providing Constructive Feedback:

"What specific examples of [Employee]'s work demonstrate
their strengths, and how can we provide constructive
feedback to help them grow?"

"How can we address [Employee]'s performance challenges in a supportive and constructive manner?"

Goal Setting and Alignment:

"What short-term and long-term goals should [Employee] set to align with the organization's objectives?"

"How can we ensure that [Employee]'s goals are SMART (Specific, Measurable, Achievable, Relevant, and Time-bound)?"

Employee Development and Growth:

"What development opportunities, such as training, mentoring, or job rotations, could help [Employee] enhance their skills and advance their career?"

"How can we support [Employee] in achieving their professional growth objectives?"

Employee Engagement and Motivation:

"What strategies can we implement to increase [Employee]'s engagement and motivation based on their performance evaluation?"

"How can we recognize [Employee]'s achievements and contributions to the team in a meaningful way?"

Team Performance and Collaboration:

"How does [Employee]'s performance impact the overall team dynamic and productivity?"

"What steps can we take to foster collaboration and teamwork between [Employee] and their colleagues?"

Performance Improvement Plan:

"What specific actions should be included in [Employee]'s performance improvement plan to address identified areas for improvement?"

"How can we monitor and support [Employee]'s progress in implementing their performance improvement plan?"

Addressing Underperformance:

"How can we communicate our concerns about [Employee]'s underperformance in a constructive and supportive manner?"

"What resources and support can we provide to [Employee] to help them overcome performance challenges?"

Celebrating Success and Encouraging High Performance:

"What initiatives can we implement to celebrate [Employee]'s achievements and encourage continued high performance?"

"How can we showcase [Employee]'s accomplishments to inspire other team members and promote a culture of excellence?"

Regular Check-ins and Ongoing Feedback:

"How can we establish a routine for regular check-ins with [Employee] to discuss their progress and provide ongoing feedback?"

"What strategies can we use to create a supportive
environment that fosters open communication between
[Employee] and their manager?"

Addressing Performance Discrepancies:

"How can we identify and address discrepancies between
[Employee]'s self-assessment and the manager's evaluation of
their performance?"

"What steps can we take to ensure that both [Employee] and
their manager have a shared understanding of performance
expectations and goals?"

Promoting a Culture of Continuous Learning:

"How can we encourage [Employee] to take ownership of their
professional development and embrace a growth mindset?"

"What strategies can we implement to promote a culture of continuous learning within the team and the organization as a whole?"

Setting SMART Goals for Improvement:

"What specific, measurable, achievable, relevant, and time-bound (SMART) goals can we set for [Employee] to address areas for improvement and enhance their performance?"

"How can we support [Employee] in working towards their SMART goals and track their progress over time?"

Leveraging AI for Performance Monitoring:

"In what ways can we utilize AI technology to more effectively monitor and analyze [Employee]'s performance data?"

"How can we ensure that the AI tools used for performance evaluation align with our organization's ethical standards and values?"

Encouraging Peer Feedback and Collaboration:

"How can we facilitate a culture of peer feedback and
collaboration to help [Employee] gain insights from
different perspectives and improve their performance?"

"What processes can we implement to make giving and
receiving peer feedback a regular part of our team's
culture?"

Aligning Performance Evaluation with Organizational Objectives:

"How can we ensure that [Employee]'s performance evaluation
is aligned with the organization's overall objectives and
priorities?"

"What steps can we take to communicate the link between
individual performance and the organization's success to
[Employee]?"

Identifying and Addressing Skill Gaps:

"How can we work with [Employee] to identify any skill gaps
that may be affecting their performance and develop an

action plan to address them?"

"What resources, such as training programs or mentorship opportunities, can we provide to help [Employee] close these skill gaps?"

Fostering Resilience and Adaptability:

"How can we support [Employee] in developing resilience and adaptability to navigate challenges and setbacks in their performance journey?"

"What strategies can we use to create a team environment that encourages learning from mistakes and fosters a growth mindset?"

Enhancing Employee Engagement and Motivation:

"What steps can we take to ensure that [Employee] is engaged and motivated to perform at their best?"

"How can we leverage AI tools to identify factors that may impact [Employee]'s engagement and motivation and develop strategies to address them?"

Conducting Effective Performance Review Conversations:

"How can we utilize AI assistance to help managers prepare for and conduct effective performance review conversations with [Employee]?"

"What strategies can we implement to ensure that performance review conversations are constructive, balanced, and focused on future growth?"d

These prompt templates can be easily adapted to various performance evaluation situations, helping managers provide actionable feedback and support employees in their growth and development.

12

Crisis Management and AI

Crisis management is an essential aspect of effective leadership, as it involves navigating unexpected challenges and ensuring the organization's resilience in the face of adversity. With the rise of AI technologies, leaders now have powerful tools at their disposal to enhance their crisis management capabilities. This chapter will explore the various ways in which AI can support and improve crisis management efforts, from predictive analytics to decision-making and post-crisis analysis.

The subchapters will delve into the following topics:

1. **Predictive Analytics for Early Warning Systems:** Understand the role of AI in developing early warning systems that can help organizations anticipate and prepare for potential crises.
2. **AI-Driven Decision Support for Crisis Management:** Learn how AI can assist leaders in making informed decisions during crises, offering valuable insights and recommendations to guide their actions.
3. **AI in Crisis Communication and Coordination:** Explore the

ways AI can facilitate communication and coordination during crises, ensuring a more effective response from all stakeholders involved.

4. **Decision-Making and Resource Allocation during Crises with AI Assistance:** Discover how AI can help leaders make better decisions regarding the allocation of resources during crises, ensuring an efficient and targeted response.

5. **Leveraging AI for Crisis Communication and Public Information Management:** Examine the role of AI in managing communication with the public and stakeholders during crises, ensuring accurate and timely information dissemination.

6. **Post-Crisis Analysis and Learning with AI:** Understand how AI can support post-crisis analysis and learning, helping organizations to identify areas for improvement and implement necessary changes.

7. **Prompt Templates for Crisis Management Scenarios:** Learn about various AI-generated prompt templates that can be used to assist leaders in managing different crisis scenarios, promoting effective decision-making and problem-solving.

By integrating AI into their crisis management strategies, leaders can better anticipate potential challenges, make informed decisions during crises, and ensure their organizations emerge stronger and more resilient. This chapter will provide a comprehensive understanding of the various ways AI can support and enhance crisis management efforts, offering practical insights for leaders navigating today's complex and rapidly changing landscape.

12.1 Predictive Analytics for Early Warning Systems

In this subchapter, we will discuss how AI-powered predictive analytics can be utilized to create early warning systems that help organizations identify potential crises before they escalate. By developing a robust early warning system, organizations can take proactive measures to mitigate risks and minimize the impact of crises.

Understanding Predictive Analytics

Predictive analytics involves analyzing historical and real-time data to identify patterns, trends, and relationships that can be used to make predictions about future events. By leveraging machine learning algorithms, AI can quickly process vast amounts of data and generate accurate predictions that can inform decision-making.

Developing Early Warning Systems with AI

An early warning system can help organizations detect potential crises in their initial stages, allowing them to take proactive measures to prevent escalation. AI can play a significant role in developing such systems, as it can continuously monitor and analyze various data sources to identify potential risks. Some key components of AI-powered early warning systems include:

1. **Data Collection:** AI algorithms can aggregate and analyze data from various sources, such as social media, news, and internal reports. This data can be used to identify patterns and trends that may signal the onset of a crisis.
2. **Real-time Analysis:** AI can process data in real-time, allowing organizations to respond to potential crises more quickly.

3. **Prediction Models:** AI can develop predictive models that generate forecasts based on historical data and current trends. These models can help organizations anticipate potential crises and take appropriate measures to mitigate risks.

4. **Alerts and Notifications:** AI-powered early warning systems can automatically send alerts and notifications to relevant stakeholders when potential risks are identified, ensuring that the right people are informed in a timely manner.

Example prompts for Developing AI-powered Early Warning Systems

```
"Develop a predictive model that can forecast potential
supply chain disruptions based on historical data and
current market trends."
```

```
"Analyze social media data to identify potential PR crises
and provide real-time alerts to the communications team."
```

```
"Create a system that continuously monitors news sources and
internal reports to detect early signs of financial fraud or
misconduct."
```

```
"Design an AI-powered tool that predicts natural disasters,
such as hurricanes and earthquakes, to enable better
preparedness and response planning."
```

```
"Implement a machine learning model to identify emerging
trends and potential risks in the industry to help
organizations adapt and stay ahead of the competition."
```

In conclusion, AI-powered predictive analytics can be a valuable tool in developing early warning systems that help organizations proactively identify and respond to potential crises. By leveraging AI's capabilities, organizations can make better-informed decisions, mitigate risks, and minimize the impact of crises on their operations.

12.2 AI-Driven Decision Support for Crisis Management

In this subchapter, we will explore the potential of AI-driven decision support systems to improve the effectiveness of crisis management. By providing timely insights and recommendations, AI can help leaders make more informed decisions during high-pressure situations, ultimately leading to better outcomes.

Understanding AI-Driven Decision Support Systems

AI-driven decision support systems (DSS) are designed to assist decision-makers by providing relevant information, analysis, and recommendations. They leverage machine learning algorithms, natural language processing, and other AI technologies to analyze complex data sets and provide actionable insights.

Key Components of AI-Driven Decision Support Systems for Crisis Management

1. **Situation Analysis:** AI algorithms can process vast amounts of data from various sources to provide a comprehensive understanding of the ongoing crisis. This includes monitoring real-time updates, analyzing historical data, and identifying trends and patterns that could impact the crisis.

2. **Scenario Modeling:** AI-driven DSS can create models of different crisis scenarios and their potential outcomes. By simulating various scenarios, decision-makers can better understand the potential consequences of their actions and make more informed choices.

3. **Decision Recommendations:** Based on the analysis of the situation and scenario modeling, AI-driven DSS can provide decision-makers with actionable recommendations. These suggestions can be ranked by their effectiveness, allowing leaders to prioritize their actions during a crisis.

4. **Continuous Learning:** As the crisis evolves, AI-driven DSS can adapt and learn from new information. This enables the system to provide updated recommendations based on the latest data and insights, ensuring that decision-makers receive the most accurate and relevant information.

Example prompts for Implementing AI-Driven Decision Support Systems in Crisis Management

"Create an AI-driven system that helps emergency response teams allocate resources more efficiently during a natural disaster, such as a hurricane or earthquake."

"Develop a decision support tool that provides real-time analysis and recommendations for managing a public health crisis, such as a pandemic."

"Design an AI-powered platform that helps corporate leaders navigate financial crises by providing insights into market trends, risk factors, and potential strategies for recovery."

"Implement a machine learning model that assists government agencies in managing political crises by predicting potential outcomes and offering policy recommendations."

"Build an AI-driven system that supports decision-making during cybersecurity incidents by identifying potential threats, assessing their impact, and suggesting appropriate countermeasures."

In summary, AI-driven decision support systems can play a crucial role in crisis management by providing timely, data-driven insights and recommendations. By leveraging AI technologies, organizations can improve their decision-making process during crises, leading to more effective responses and better overall outcomes.

12.3 AI in Crisis Communication and Coordination

In this subchapter, we will delve into the importance of effective communication and coordination during crises and how AI can enhance these aspects. From analyzing and disseminating information to facilitating collaboration among stakeholders, AI technologies can significantly improve the way organizations handle crisis situations.

AI-Powered Crisis Communication Systems

AI can be utilized to develop crisis communication systems that automatically analyze and disseminate information. These systems can:

1. **Monitor social media and other online platforms:** Detect early signs of a crisis, such as unusual spikes in specific keywords or phrases related to the event.
2. **Aggregate and process data from various sources:** News outlets, government agencies, and social media, to provide a comprehensive and up-to-date overview of the crisis.
3. **Automatically generate and distribute crisis-related updates:** Ensuring relevant stakeholders stay informed and aligned.

AI-Enabled Collaboration and Coordination Tools

AI can also be used to create collaboration and coordination tools that facilitate seamless communication among crisis management teams. Key features of these tools include:

1. **Real-time translation capabilities**, allowing team members who speak different languages to communicate effectively.

2. **Sentiment analysis and emotion detection** to gauge the public's reaction to the crisis and adapt communication strategies accordingly.

3. **Automated scheduling and task management** to ensure that team members are aware of their responsibilities and deadlines.

Example prompts for Implementing AI in Crisis Communication and Coordination

"Design an AI-powered system that monitors social media for early signs of a public health crisis and alerts relevant authorities and organizations."

"Develop an AI-driven communication platform that automatically translates messages between crisis response team members who speak different languages."

"Create a machine learning model that predicts the public's reaction to crisis-related news and adjusts communication strategies accordingly."

```
"Implement an AI-assisted task management system that helps
crisis management teams coordinate their efforts more
efficiently."
```

```
"Build an AI-powered tool that generates and distributes
real-time updates on a crisis situation to relevant
stakeholders, such as government agencies, first responders,
and the public."
```

Overall, AI can significantly enhance communication and coordination during crises by providing real-time insights, facilitating collaboration among stakeholders, and automating key aspects of information dissemination. By harnessing the power of AI, organizations can improve their crisis response efforts, ultimately minimizing the negative impact of these events on society.

12.4 Decision-Making and Resource Allocation during Crises with AI Assistance

In this subchapter, we will discuss how AI can aid in decision-making and resource allocation during crisis situations. With the help of AI technologies, organizations can make more informed decisions and allocate resources more effectively, ultimately improving their ability to manage and resolve crises.

AI-Driven Decision Support Systems

AI-driven decision support systems can help organizations make more informed decisions during crises by providing valuable insights and recommendations. These systems can:

1. Analyze vast amounts of data from various sources, such as social media, news outlets, and sensors, to provide a comprehensive understanding of the crisis situation.
2. Use machine learning algorithms to identify patterns and trends in the data, allowing organizations to predict the potential impacts of different courses of action.
3. Generate recommendations based on the analyzed data, helping decision-makers weigh the pros and cons of each option.

Optimizing Resource Allocation with AI

AI technologies can also be utilized to optimize resource allocation during crises. By analyzing data and making predictions, AI-powered tools can:

1. **Determine the most efficient way to allocate resources**, such as personnel, equipment, and supplies, based on the specific needs and constraints of the crisis situation.
2. **Monitor the effectiveness of resource allocation strategies** in real-time and make adjustments as needed.
3. **Forecast the potential future needs for resources**, allowing organizations to plan and prepare accordingly.

Example prompts for Implementing AI in Decision-Making and Resource Allocation during Crises

```
"Develop an AI-powered decision support system that analyzes
data from multiple sources and provides recommendations for
crisis management strategies."
```

235

"Create a machine learning model that predicts the potential impacts of different resource allocation strategies during a crisis."

"Design an AI-driven tool that optimizes the allocation of emergency response personnel and equipment during a natural disaster."

"Implement an AI-powered system that monitors the effectiveness of resource allocation strategies during a crisis and makes real-time adjustments as needed."

"Build an AI-assisted forecasting tool that predicts future resource needs during prolonged crisis situations."

In summary, AI can play a crucial role in enhancing decision-making and resource allocation during crises. By providing valuable insights, predictions, and recommendations, AI technologies can help organizations make more informed decisions and allocate resources more effectively, ultimately improving their ability to manage and resolve crisis situations.

12.5 Leveraging AI for Crisis Communication and Public Information Management

Effective communication and public information management are crucial aspects of crisis management. In this subchapter, we will explore how AI can be used to enhance crisis communication and manage public information during emergencies.

AI-Powered Social Media Monitoring and Analysis

Social media platforms can be a valuable source of information during crises. AI technologies can be employed to monitor and analyze social media data, helping organizations to:

1. **Identify emerging crises** and assess their potential impacts.
2. **Track the public's sentiment** and concerns regarding the crisis.
3. **Detect and address misinformation and rumors** that may exacerbate the situation.

Natural Language Processing for Public Information Management

Natural language processing (NLP) is an AI technology that can be used to process and analyze large volumes of text data. NLP can be applied in crisis communication and public information management to:

1. **Automatically classify and prioritize incoming information**, such as reports from the public or emergency responders.
2. **Generate summaries and insights from large volumes of textual data**, making it easier for decision-makers to process and understand the information.

3. **Automate the generation of public announcements and updates**, ensuring that consistent and accurate information is shared with the public.

Chatbots and Virtual Assistants for Crisis Communication

AI-powered chatbots and virtual assistants can be deployed to facilitate communication between organizations and the public during crises. These tools can:

1. **Provide immediate and accurate responses to common questions and concerns.**
2. **Collect and analyze feedback from the public**, enabling organizations to better understand and address their needs.
3. **Reduce the workload on human staff**, allowing them to focus on more complex tasks and decision-making.

Example prompts for Implementing AI in Crisis Communication and Public Information Management

```
"Develop an AI-driven social media monitoring and analysis
tool to track public sentiment and misinformation during
crises."
```

```
"Create an NLP-based system that automatically classifies
and prioritizes incoming crisis-related information."
```

"Design a chatbot or virtual assistant that can answer common questions and provide accurate information to the public during emergencies."

"Implement an AI-powered system that generates public announcements and updates based on real-time crisis information."

"Build a platform that combines AI technologies to enhance communication and public information management during crisis situations."

In conclusion, AI technologies can significantly improve crisis communication and public information management. By leveraging AI-powered social media monitoring, natural language processing, and chatbots, organizations can effectively manage information, communicate with the public, and make more informed decisions during emergencies.

12.6 Post-Crisis Analysis and Learning with AI

Once a crisis has been resolved, it is essential for organizations to analyze the event, evaluate their response, and learn from the experience to improve future crisis management. AI can play a significant role in post-crisis analysis and learning, helping organizations to extract insights and develop more effective strategies for future emergencies.

AI-Enabled Data Analysis and Pattern Recognition

AI technologies can be employed to analyze large volumes of data generated during a crisis. By identifying patterns and trends, AI can help organizations to:

1. **Understand the factors** that contributed to the crisis and its escalation.
2. **Evaluate the effectiveness** of their crisis response strategies.
3. **Identify areas for improvement** in their crisis management processes.

Predictive Modeling for Crisis Prevention

Using machine learning algorithms, AI can develop predictive models based on historical crisis data. These models can be used to:

1. **Forecast the likelihood of future crises**, allowing organizations to take preventative measures.
2. **Assess the potential impact of various crisis scenarios**, enabling organizations to prioritize resources and plan accordingly.
3. **Simulate the effectiveness of different response strategies**, providing valuable insights for decision-makers.

Natural Language Processing for Sentiment Analysis and Lessons Learned

AI-powered natural language processing can be used to analyze textual data, such as reports, news articles, and social media posts, to evaluate public sentiment and extract lessons learned during the crisis. NLP can help organizations to:

1. **Assess the effectiveness** of their communication strategies and

public relations efforts during the crisis.

2. **Identify the public's concerns and priorities**, guiding the development of more effective crisis response plans.

3. **Extract key lessons and best practices** from the crisis, informing future crisis management strategies.

Example prompts for Post-Crisis Analysis and Learning with AI

"Develop an AI-powered data analysis system to identify patterns and trends in crisis events and evaluate the effectiveness of crisis response strategies."

"Create a predictive modeling tool that forecasts the likelihood and impact of future crises, guiding resource allocation and planning."

"Design an NLP-based system for sentiment analysis and lessons learned extraction from textual data related to crisis events."

"Implement an AI-driven platform that combines data
analysis, predictive modeling, and natural language
processing for comprehensive post-crisis analysis and
learning."

"Build a knowledge base of best practices and lessons
learned from past crises, using AI technologies to
facilitate continuous improvement in crisis management."

In summary, AI technologies can significantly enhance post-crisis analysis and learning, enabling organizations to extract valuable insights from crisis data, evaluate their response strategies, and develop more effective plans for future emergencies. By incorporating AI-driven data analysis, predictive modeling, and natural language processing, organizations can continuously improve their crisis management capabilities and build resilience against future challenges.

12.7 Prompt Templates for Crisis Management Scenarios

In this subchapter, we provide prompt templates that can help guide AI applications in various crisis management scenarios. These templates can be customized and adapted to suit specific organizational needs and situations. Here are ten prompt templates with descriptions of their purposes:

Analyzing Critical Factors and Recommendations

"Analyze and identify the critical factors that contributed to the [crisis] and provide recommendations to mitigate the risk of such an event in the future."

This prompt helps to identify the root causes of a crisis and suggests potential strategies to prevent similar situations from happening again.

Crisis Communication Plan Development

"Develop a crisis communication plan to address the concerns and questions of [stakeholders] during the [crisis] effectively."

This prompt assists in creating a communication strategy for stakeholders during a crisis, ensuring transparency and clarity.

Assessing Crisis Response Strategies

"Assess the effectiveness of our current crisis response strategies for [crisis] and suggest improvements or alternative approaches."

This prompt evaluates the success of existing crisis management strategies and recommends enhancements or new methods.

Creating Predictive Models for Crisis Forecasting

"Using historical data, create a predictive model to forecast the likelihood of a [crisis] occurring within the next [time frame]."

This prompt helps develop a predictive model using past data to estimate the probability of a future crisis, allowing for better preparedness.

Evaluating Potential Impact and Risk Mitigation

> "Evaluate the potential impact of [crisis] on our
> organization's operations, finances, and reputation, and
> recommend measures to minimize these risks."

This prompt assesses the possible consequences of a crisis on different aspects of an organization and suggests ways to minimize potential damage.

Designing AI-Powered Early Warning Systems

> "Design an AI-powered early warning system to detect early
> signs of [crisis] and alert the relevant teams for prompt
> action."

This prompt focuses on developing an AI-driven system to detect early indicators of a crisis, enabling faster responses and mitigating potential harm.

Developing Comprehensive Crisis Management Plans

> "Develop a comprehensive crisis management plan for
> [crisis], outlining the roles and responsibilities of key
> personnel, communication strategies, and resource
> allocation."

This prompt guides the creation of a thorough crisis management plan, detailing responsibilities, communication, and resources needed during a crisis.

Analyzing Social Media Sentiment

"Analyze social media sentiment during the [crisis] to gauge public opinion and assess the effectiveness of our public relations efforts."

This prompt examines social media sentiment to understand public perception and evaluate the success of PR strategies during a crisis.

Simulating Crisis Scenarios for Resilience Testing

"Simulate different crisis scenarios to test the resilience of our organization's infrastructure, systems, and processes, and recommend necessary improvements."

This prompt involves simulating various crisis scenarios to evaluate an organization's resilience and suggesting enhancements to infrastructure, systems, and processes.

Compiling Post-Crisis Reports

"Compile a post-crisis report for [crisis], summarizing the lessons learned, areas of improvement, and recommendations for future crisis management."

This prompt assists in creating a comprehensive post-crisis report, highlighting key takeaways, improvement areas, and recommendations for handling future crises.

Monitoring and Analyzing Real-Time Data

"Monitor and analyze real-time data during the [crisis] to
identify trends, emerging issues, and potential
opportunities for intervention."

This prompt aims to leverage real-time data analysis to understand
ongoing trends and pinpoint areas where timely intervention can make
a difference during a crisis.

Identifying Vulnerable Aspects of Supply Chains

"Identify the most vulnerable aspects of our supply chain
during the [crisis] and develop contingency plans to
minimize disruptions."

This prompt evaluates the weak points of a supply chain during a crisis
and proposes contingency plans to reduce potential disruptions.

Reviewing Legal and Regulatory Implications

"Review the legal and regulatory implications of the
[crisis] on our organization and recommend appropriate
actions to ensure compliance."

This prompt examines legal and regulatory consequences resulting
from a crisis and suggests actions to maintain compliance.

Analyzing Remote Work Infrastructure

> "Analyze the effectiveness of our remote work infrastructure during the [crisis] and provide recommendations for improvements or expansions."

This prompt assesses the remote work infrastructure's performance during a crisis and recommends enhancements or expansions as needed.

Evaluating Psychological Impact on Employees

> "Evaluate the psychological impact of the [crisis] on our employees and suggest supportive measures to maintain their well-being and productivity."

This prompt explores the mental health effects of a crisis on employees and offers supportive initiatives to promote well-being and productivity

Designing Crisis Management Training Programs

> "Design a training program to better prepare our team members for handling [crisis] situations and adapting to rapidly changing circumstances."

This prompt focuses on creating a training program to equip team members with the skills and knowledge needed to manage crises effectively.

Assessing Economic Implications and Strategy

"Assess the economic implications of the [crisis] on our
industry and create a strategy to maintain competitiveness
and market share."

This prompt evaluates the economic impact of a crisis on the industry and formulates a strategy to preserve an organization's competitiveness and market presence.

Identifying Potential Partnerships and Collaborations

"Identify potential partnerships or collaborations that can
help our organization navigate the [crisis] more effectively
and strengthen our resilience."

This prompt searches for potential partners or collaborators to enhance an organization's ability to manage crises and build resilience.

Creating Knowledge Bases for Crisis Management

"Create a knowledge base of best practices, lessons learned,
and resources related to [crisis] management for future
reference and ongoing improvement."

This prompt establishes a repository of valuable information on crisis management, including best practices, lessons learned, and useful resources for continuous improvement.

Developing Post-Crisis Recovery Plans

```
"Develop a post-crisis recovery plan that outlines the
necessary steps to restore normal operations, regain market
position, and address any lingering effects of the [crisis]."
```

This prompt guides the creation of a post-crisis recovery plan, detailing the steps needed to return to normal operations, reclaim market standing, and address any residual consequences of the crisis.

In conclusion, this subchapter provided a variety of prompt templates designed to help organizations navigate crisis management scenarios. By utilizing these templates, leaders can gain insights into crucial aspects of crisis management, including communication, resource allocation, risk management, customer satisfaction, and decision-making processes. The templates also assist in evaluating organizational preparedness, maintaining strong customer relationships, and ensuring supply chain resilience. It is essential for organizations to adapt these templates to their specific context and needs, enabling them to effectively address crises and minimize their negative impacts.

13

Conclusion

A s we conclude this comprehensive guide to leveraging AI in leadership, it is essential to reflect on the key takeaways and consider the steps leaders can take to incorporate AI into their management practices.

Integrating AI into your leadership toolkit:

The primary goal of this guide has been to demonstrate the many ways AI can enhance and support leadership efforts across various domains, including communication, decision-making, problem-solving, collaboration, financial management, innovation, ethical leadership, performance evaluation, and crisis management. By incorporating AI into your leadership toolkit, you can streamline processes, make data-driven decisions, and foster a more innovative and resilient organization.

Preparing for future advancements in AI:

As AI technology continues to evolve, leaders must stay informed about the latest developments and adapt their strategies accordingly. Embracing a growth mindset and being open to change will help leaders remain agile and prepared for the potential challenges and opportunities that emerging technologies bring. Continuous learning, upskilling, and reskilling efforts should be encouraged within the organization to ensure that teams are equipped with the knowledge and skills required to work effectively alongside AI tools.

Embracing AI as a strategic partner in leadership:

AI has the potential to become a strategic partner for leaders, offering valuable insights and support in the decision-making process. By treating AI as a valuable resource and not merely a tool, leaders can optimize their efforts and strengthen their organizations. Establishing a strong partnership with AI involves building trust, understanding the capabilities and limitations of the technology, and promoting a collaborative environment where humans and machines work together to achieve common goals.

In conclusion, AI offers immense potential to revolutionize leadership and management practices. By embracing AI as an essential component of the leadership toolkit, being prepared for future advancements, and fostering a collaborative environment between humans and AI, leaders can unlock new levels of efficiency, innovation, and growth for their organizations.

Also by Saif Hussaini

Mastering GPT-4: The Ultimate Guide to Harnessing the Power of AI. "Mastering GPT-4: The Ultimate Guide to Harnessing the Power of AI" - Delve into the captivating world of GPT-4, the groundbreaking AI model that's revolutionizing the way we work and interact. This essential guide covers everything from the model's architecture to real-world applications, equipping you with the knowledge to stay ahead of the curve in the AI revolution. Unleash the full potential of GPT-4 and transform your projects and career with this must-read resource!

ChatGPT Toolkit for HR Recruiters: Ready-to-Use Prompts for the Modern Recruiter

Discover the power of AI in HR and recruitment with "ChatGPT Toolkit for HR Recruiters: Ready-to-Use Prompts for the Modern Recruiter." In this groundbreaking guide, you'll find a collection of AI-generated prompts that will help you transform and streamline your daily tasks in recruitment. Covering a wide range of topics from talent sourcing and candidate screening to onboarding and compliance, this book is an essential resource for HR professionals who want to stay ahead of the curve in an increasingly AI-driven world. Unlock the potential of AI in your recruitment processes and enhance your HR toolkit with this must-have guide.

Made in the USA
Coppell, TX
21 April 2024

31575013R00144